The Cry for Peace

The Cry for Peace

Andrea Riccardi

Published by New City Press
202 Comforter Blvd., Hyde Park, NY 12538
www.newcitypress.com
©2024 New City Press (English translation)

The Cry for Peace
Andrea Riccardi

Translated by Caroline Swinton from the original Italian *Il Grido della Pace*
© 2023 Edizioni San Paolo s.r.l.
Piazza Soncino 5 – 20092 Cinisello Balsamo (Milano) – Italy
www.edizionisanpaolo.it

ISBN: 978-1-56548-622-5 (paper)
ISBN: 978-1-56548-626-3 (e-book)

Library of Congress Control Number: 2024941324

Printed in the United States of America

Contents

One
The Cry for Peace
Another War 9
A Country Familiar with Suffering 12
Lost Peace: A New International Order
    That Has Not Come About 16
The Justification of War 19
The Legacy of War 22
The Loss of Peace in Syria 25
The Destruction of a World 29
The Drama of Ukraine 33
The Uprising against Being Irrelevant 36
A Vision of Peace 40

Two
Remembering Wars, the Hope for Peace
Remembering Wars 45
A Period That Is Familiar with War 47
Why History Is Necessary 50
The Globalized World 53
The Church, a Source of Humanity and Peace 55
Europe 59

Three
The Culture of Hatred and Nationalism
Hatred Is Old, but Also Very Present Today 62
The Nation and Nationalism 64
The Nationalization of Cities 68
The Nation and the Teaching of Hatred 71
Overcoming Hatred in the Global World 75

Four

The Resistance of the Righteous in the Darkness of the Holocaust

    An Event in History Never to Be Forgotten 78
    A European History. 81
    The Collaborators of Evil 85
    The Resistance of the Righteous. 88

Five

Christians and the Future of Europe

    Fear of the Future. 96
    Community and Family Ties in Europe Are Being
        Loosened in Favor of Individualism.. 98
    The Gospel Frees Us from Fear, Senility and Conformism. . . 100
    Nation, Nationalism, and the
        Weakened Power of Christianity 102
    The Prophecy of Gratuitousness 105
    An Ecumenical Civilization: Living with the Others,
        for the Other and for the Poorest 107

Six

Peace, Fraternity and Dialogue among Religions

    The Advocacy of Religions and Pope John Paul II 112
    From Dialogue to Fraternity. 114
    A Unique Event or a Process of Fraternity? 116
    The Clash between Civilizations and the
        Crisis of Ecumenical Ideals. 118
    War and Peace 120
    The Steps Taken by Religions 121
    The Fraternity of Religions and the Future of the World. 124

Seven

Sister Churches, Brother Nations

    The Origin of a Dream 126
    Ecumenical Passion: the Rise and Fall of a Unitive Sentiment 129

The Crisis of Ecumenism 133
Christians in a Non-ecumenical History 136

Eight
"How Could You Be My Enemy?"

The Drama of World War I............................ 141
The Pope, Peace, and Peace Movements 144
Popular Piety and Humanism of the Poor 148
Peace, Protestantism, and Christian Unity............... 150
Peace and Christian Unity 153

Nine
A Passionate Seeker of Peace: Giorgio La Pira

The Historiography of the Depths 158
Beyond the Cold War, Conflicts, Clashes of Civilizations ... 161
Attraction, Dialogue, Building Bridges.................. 167
A Christian and a Passionate Seeker of Peace............. 172

Ten
Community: From Me to Us

From the Dream of Us to the Reality of Me 177
Who Is My Neighbor?................................ 180
The Great Change and Subsequent Reactions 185
A Community Revolution? 189

Eleven
Visions Beyond the Wall of the Impossible

Humanity Suffers Mostly from a Lack of Vision 195
With No Visions but with Limitless Horizons 198
Regaining History Opens Us to the Vision of the Future 202

One

The Cry for Peace

Another War

Edgar Morin recently published a small book called *Di guerra in guerra* (From War to War), written with undiminished passion despite the fact that, at the time of writing, he was 101 years old, and had seen a great many wars.[1] In fact, one understands the value of peace, above all when it is lacking, like the absence of air. Morin, a theorist of complexity, stated an undeniable truth: "The more war escalates, the more difficult and urgent peace becomes. Let us prevent a world war. It would be worse than the previous one."[2]

With the continuation of the war in Ukraine, the possibility of peace seems to be moving further and further away, at the risk of more countries getting involved and the still present threat of an atomic bomb. Faced with this ongoing war, a reflection on peace may seem anachronistic. However, it is important to develop this thought because it would be absurd if a peaceful future really were an anachronism. Nonetheless, peace is actually perceived as less and less feasible, almost as though it were a utopian objective. It seems incredible, but over the years, the perception of the importance of peace, of the need for it in human society has become uncertain.

Far too many people are paying the price of the peace currently lost. I am thinking in particular about Ukraine,

---

1. Edgar Morin, *Di guerra in guerra. Dal 1940 all'Ucraina invasa*, trans. Susanna Lazzari (Milan: Raffaello Cortina Editore, 2023).
2. Ibid, 104.

a country of almost forty-five million inhabitants. I love Ukraine, which I have known since it was part of the Soviet Union. At that time, I had the opportunity, in particular in Galicia, a region in the west of the country, to meet groups of people who longed for their independence. I remember, again during the Soviet rule, a demonstration for independence in Kiev, and people waving the Ukrainian flag that we are so familiar with today. Ukraine became independent in 1991, and for a short time was a free country with a complex relationship with the nearby Russian Federation, since a lot of people spoke Russian and many were pro-Russia, whereas many others were attracted to Europe and the West. Putin's attack on the country has had the opposite effect to what he hoped for: the surprisingly strong Ukrainian resistance has unified almost the whole country.

Ukraine has suffered dreadfully for years, and it is important to know the history of a population because every nation is a child of its history. When I see the masses of Ukrainian refugees fleeing the war and when I think about the country's history, I am reminded of the words of the prophet Isaiah, "a man who knows well the suffering" (Isaiah 53:3). Just thinking of the terrible twentieth century in Ukraine is sufficient to be aware of this.

To start with there was the civil war after the Bolshevik Revolution; the one between 1918 and 1921 between the Soviets and independent Ukraine; then the 1920s with the anti-Semitic pogroms; the violence of the Soviet security service against the separatists, against the Christians, and the intellectuals, and the middle class resulting in the death of thousands of people. In 1932, a famine caused by the new economic policies gripped Ukraine, and four million people died. Travelers to the country told of dreadful scenes, even of cannibalism, as the population was starving. Stalin refused to help Ukrainians and left them to die. The Holodomor (a combination of two Ukrainian words: hunger and killing) was recognized by the Ukrainian state and a number of other countries as a genocide.

In 1941, in the middle of World War II, Hitler attacked Soviet Ukraine and reached Kiev. Between three and five million people lost their lives, and a vast number of buildings were destroyed, including the cathedral of the country's most symbolic monument, the Kiev Monastery of the Caves. That year, between September 29 and 30, over thirty thousand Jews were exterminated in the Babi Yar gorges, near the capital. Altogether 1.6 million Ukrainian Jews were assassinated. Those who fled to the forests were killed by Polish and Ukrainian resistance fighters. A significant number of Ukrainians participated in the massacre of the Jews, and this assisted Nazi operations.

The life of the Jews of Eastern Europe was very tough during the first half of the twentieth century, and they accounted for one-third of those exterminated by the madness of the Holocaust. However, even before World War II their life was extremely difficult. Jeffrey Veidlinger, an American historian, wrote a dramatic book, *In the Midst of Civilized Europe: The 1918–1921 Pogroms in Ukraine and the Onset of the Holocaust* in which he documented the pogroms against the Jews that took place in Ukraine and in Poland, as one of the origins of the slaughter of the Eastern European Jews.[3] Veidlinger wrote, "The Germans took strategic and deliberate advantage of the existing anti-Semitic sentiments and used the local motives to unleash another wave of massacre and stage a copy of what was executed by the previous generations."[4]

---

3. Jeffrey Veidlinger, *In the Midst of Civilized Europe: The 1918–1921 Pogroms in Ukraine and the Onset of the Holocaust* (New York: Macmillan, 2021).
4. Ibid, 374–375.

The Ukrainians suffered immensely during the Second World War. The Nazis forced men and women to carry out hard labor, and when the Soviets took over the country again, the result for what was considered a Soviet Union Republic was disastrous: between three and five million people had died and 770 towns and eighteen thousand villages had been destroyed. At the end of the war, the country fell under heavy-handed Soviet control again. The repression was harsh, not only among the groups of separatists, but also in the Greek-Catholic Church, which had been linked with Rome for centuries and was mainly based in Galicia. It was viciously forced to become part of the Russian Orthodox Church, while all its bishops were deported to the gulags and some of the clergy and the churchgoers were arrested.

A Country Familiar with Suffering

Ukraine is historically a multiethnic country with a strong Ukrainian majority and is becoming increasingly conscious of its identity. In its thirty years of independence, despite its fragility, and amid great political and economic difficulties, Ukrainian democracy has nonetheless developed its own personality. After all, the name Ukraine means a frontier or a border country. Jürgen Habermas said, "Amongst the European nations that were lagging behind, Ukraine has arrived as the last one. Probably it is still a nation in the making."[5] As a reaction to the devastating attack by the Russians, on February 24, 2022, the national identity has become more compact, since even Russian speakers have joined the Ukrainian resistance.

---

5. Jürgen Habermas, *A Plea for Negotiations*, "Süddeutsche Zeitung," Jürgen Habermas: A Plea for Negotiations – SZ.de (sueddeutsche.de), February 14, 2023.

Ukrainians were living in Italian and European towns well before the war too. In Italy there were already 230,000 Ukrainian women, often employed as household help or to look after the elderly. They were strong women, who with their work supported their families at home. Their work illustrates how important immigrants are for Italy's future. It shows us how we Italians are unlikely to even have a future if we do not open up and welcome immigrants.[6]

When the war broke out, at the border between Ukraine and Slovakia, I met Ukrainian women fleeing their country and taking their children and the elderly with them. They were strong, dignified women representing an important aspect of their country. The men obviously could not go with them because they had to stay and fight.

Encounters with other people (in this case Ukrainian women), open us up, if only we have the patience to listen and talk to them. Thanks to them, we can find out about previously unknown worlds. In our excessively self-absorbed world, despite being bombarded by so much news, getting to know immigrant Ukrainian women reveals a universe of stories, hardship, and pain. The prophets of Israel taught us: "Who is a wise man? The one who learns from other men." These women too, despite the humble work they do, have so much to teach us; they can explain a lot about suffering, both that of days long past and of recent ones as well. They can tell us, in a very personal way, about the pain of their country through the experience of their own families. They talk about the pain of having lost their homes and about their relatives who have been affected by the war. I met some women in Kiev who came from Donbass, and they told me, "We had to run away. We got on a bus, and we did not even

---

6. Andrea Riccardi and Lucio Caracciolo, *Accogliere* (Milan: Piemme, 2023).

know where it was going!" Understandably, many Ukrainian women who fled abroad closely follow the news on the war, which is reported extensively by the international media.

I was impressed by the welcome given to Ukrainians by people from all walks of life, from the very beginning of the invasion. In fact, many European towns, sometimes even small towns, become cosmopolitan, thanks to the presence of immigrants. They bring their history with them, even if we do not often ask them any questions because they seem to be unimportant. The Russian poet Yevgeny Yevtushenkio whose mother was from Ukraine and whose father was Russian, wrote:

> If someone lived without attracting notice
> and made a friend of their obscurity –
> then their uniqueness was precisely this.
> Their very plainness made them interesting.[7]

Meeting the sons and daughters of other populations broadens the mind and opens the heart, and it also limits the arrogant and selfish ego. Pope Francis, in his encyclical *Fratelli tutti*, teaches us: "The ability to sit down and listen to others, typical of interpersonal encounters, is paradigmatic of the welcoming attitude shown by those who transcend narcissism and accept others, caring for them and welcoming them into their lives."[8]

During the Russian attack on Ukraine, around ten million Ukrainians came to Western Europe, some of whom returned home after a few months. Much of Western Europe (starting with Poland, which admitted most of them) has

---

7. Yevgeny Yevtushenko, https://www.theguardian.com/books/2017/may/06/saturday-poem-there-are-no-boring-people-yevgeny-yevtushenko-boris-dralyuk
8. Francis, Encyclical Letter *Fratelli Tutti*, Fratelli tutti (3 October 2020) | Francis (vatican.va) no. 48.

Ukrainians living there. This is one of the many dramas caused by war: the depopulation and the forced exile of large numbers of people.

Ukraine is paying a very heavy price and if we are talking about peace, it is above all for Ukraine, whose land has been devastated and whose children are scattered across Europe. The country's infrastructure has also been destroyed: five million Ukrainians are homeless, and 2.4 million homes have been damaged; 1,206 health centers and 2,300 schools have been hit, 438 of them razed to the ground. This war has not only caused destruction but has also involved widespread cruelty. There are at least six million internally displaced people, and many are missing.

Ukraine is the poorest country in Europe: its economy was reduced by 30 percent in 2022. Twenty million Ukrainians have lost their income, and sixteen million people are out of work. The World Health Organization says that around nine million people in Ukraine risk suffering from mental illness. Moreover, in 2023, over 17.5 million Ukrainians needed humanitarian aid. However, after the initial enthusiasm, there is a decrease in aid sent, partly because countries in Europe are going through a difficult period due to the increase in the cost of gas and fuel resulting from the sanctions imposed on Russia.[9] This is precisely why, since the winter of 2023, Ukraine has been experiencing a real humanitarian emergency.

Although the Russian attacks are being averted and most of the country is being spared from the invasion, the Ukrainian people are still paying a very heavy price. It is not easy to count the casualties because both sides keep the information related to the war secret, but it is said that

---

9. As of the moment, Western European nations have solidified their support for Ukraine.

between Russians and Ukrainians, around two hundred thousand people have died in action. I have seen the sections of Ukrainian cemeteries where soldiers killed at war are buried and, regardless of how many flags and flowers there are, they cannot hide the pain and sorrow. One's thoughts go out to everyone, especially to young people, a generation that, unlike their European peers, have a personal experience of the war and have seen their dreams for the future swept away by it. Young Ukrainians have been increasingly determined to defend their country from Putin and his armed forces' attacks, whereas many of the Russian soldiers appear to be demotivated despite Moscow's massive propaganda. The death of young Ukrainians and Russians makes one ask an unavoidable question: why was their fate so different from that of young Europeans? The answer is, "Because there is no more peace in their country." Is that too simple an answer?

Lost Peace: A New International Order That Has Not Come About

The question posed above is not in fact easy to answer, because we are living in a time of "terrible simplifiers," an effective expression of the nineteenth century historian Jacob Burckhardt, that indicates a tendency, which by now is firmly consolidated in the news and in the social media. War leads to a militarized way of thinking, it makes one take sides, and encourages or rather forces one to simplify everything. Instead, the complexity of the world and the different histories throughout the world make it clear that a simplification of the facts should be resisted because, by simplifying them, nothing is explained, yet one is reassured. Above all, in this way, it is possible to avoid asking oneself difficult questions.

To achieve peace, one has to understand the populations of a country and the people who lead them, and this is not easy at all. Polarization, which is typical of journalism and of politics, encourages simplifications, and they are almost always in conflict with each other. Moisés Naim says, "Relentless demonization of enemies is the dynamics of fandom."[10] Simplifications, polarizations, and fandom go together. This is not enough to be able to understand the reality of our times, not because one has to be a refined geopolitician or a learned historian, but because a sense of its complexity is necessary in order to understand history, above all contemporary history. Complexity is fundamental in people who cultivate a thinking approach to reality and do not close themselves in the militarization of thinking. Complexity is the great lesson that educates one to carry out research and strive for freedom. However, as Naim said, the dynamics of fandom, refusing dialogue and complex thought, is typical of authoritarian and populist regimes and can also lead to the breakdown of democracies.

Why has the world lost peace? This phenomenon started a long time ago. With the advance of the globalized world, after 1989, with the strong emergence of national identities, but also of transnational powers and networks, the contemporary world acquired such a degree of complexity that it is not easy to navigate. The Cold War split the world roughly into two empires, with two ideologies and two markets.... It was not, in fact, so clear-cut, but it was easy to opt for one side or the other. Today, however, to orient oneself, one needs endless information, culture, thinking, and an ability to be critical. Therefore, one tends to spontaneously close oneself in one's own little bubble, or in one's tribal provincialism, perhaps despising those who are not part of

---

10. Moisés Naim, *The Revenge of Power. How Autocrats are Reinventing Politics for the 21st Century* (New York: St. Martin's Press, 2022), xvii.

it, or else relying on culturally inadequate but personally reassuring simplifications.

After 1989, globalization was discussed at length, and its great opportunities and limits were highlighted, but basically public opinion generally believed in a kind of global opportunism. This meant that the markets, financial transactions, networking, communications, and transport would be unified, and, with the decrease of borders, this would all gradually create a prosperous world, in which democracy would make progress, and people would live together peacefully throughout the world. This was going to be the "end of history" predicted by Francis Fukuyama, who in the end had to admit he had been wrong.[11] Over the last thirty years, international relations have not moved in the providential direction of peace and democracy that was hoped for and expected as the natural outcome of globalization.

The events of September 11, 2001, brought to light the clashes between civilizations and religions in conflict with the globalization of the markets. This is the well-known theory of the "clash of civilizations," in which Samuel Huntington aimed to explain the ethnic and religious reactions to Western globalization, considered invasive. At the same time, strong national identities that the West was not really aware of, were emerging throughout the whole world, as in, for example, the Balkans (following the breakup of Yugoslavia) or in the former Soviet Union (Ukraine). The contested emergence of some countries caused bloody conflicts that still have not been completely resolved. The world did not seize the great opportunities in 1989 to build new, stable, international relations. One thinks of the openness of Russia toward a new European and world order after the

---

11. Francis Fukuyama, *The End of History and the Last Man* (Washington, D.C.: Free Press, 1992).

trauma of the end of the USSR. (The end of empires often result in conflicting reactions, as happened in Turkey under Atatürk, after the end of the Ottoman Empire), and also of the emergence of China, as a decisive international player alongside the United States.

December 11, 2001, is an important date too because that is when China became a member of the World Trade Organization. The West thought that opening up the world market would lead to spreading values and the implication of freedom and human rights. However, it did not happen. In the following twenty years, imports into Europe from China increased from 80 to 383 billion dollars, but China still has a single-party political system. In fact, today the Chinese model presents itself as a viable system for other countries too. Moreover, democracies do not appear to be particularly successful models, and actually they often find themselves in trouble, whereas new populist, Bonapartist, "*democratures*," or illiberal democracies (as Eduardo Galeano called governments characterized by authoritarianism under a democratic guise) are asserting themselves.

The Justification of War

In 2003, a great peace movement brought together millions of people in protests against the Iraq War. Despite the dreadful attacks of September 11, 2001 (and Al Qaida's responsibility for Islamist terrorism), and the spreading of the theory of the clash of civilizations and religions, there was still a deep awareness of the horrors of war, which had developed in more than one generation of people who recognized the value of peace.

John Paul II, who was born in 1920 and was praised for his commitment to the liberation of Eastern Europe from communism, was strongly opposed to the military intervention in Iraq. In March 2003, he said, "I belong to the generation which lived during and survived World War II. It is my duty to tell all the young people, all those younger than myself, who did not have the same experience, no more war!"[12] The poet David Maria Turoldo, who was born in 1916 and was not yet thirty during the World War, also challenged young people saying, "Do not follow the road we did. I am not ashamed of my participation in the war since I only fought in the resistance, which meant a human being against an inhuman one."[13] The generation that lived through World War II still remembers the horrors of war, even though their countries were liberated from the Nazi regime and from fascism.

Soldiers have a keen sense of peace, knowing they fight in order to achieve it. Yitzhak Rabin, a great politician, and an Israeli soldier, who fought for his country, had the political courage to negotiate the Oslo Accords, which created the basis for peaceful coexistence between Israelis and Palestinians. Rabin won the Nobel Peace Prize together with Shimon Peres, his former political rival, and the Palestinian leader Yasser Arafat. Unfortunately, in 1995, Yitzhak Rabin was killed by a Jewish extremist.

In the twenty-first century, there was the arrival of new generations of people born long after World War II. What has become even more crucial to the passing of whole generations is the passing of the survivors of the Holocaust who played a decisive role in the development of Western consciousness regarding its responsibility toward history. One should be grateful to them for having talked and written

---

12. These words were spoken spontaneously during the recitation of the Angelus on March 16, 2003.
13. David M. Turoldo, *La guerra sconfitta di Dio* (Treviso: Colibrì 1993), 35.

about their experiences and remember not only their suffering but also their generous efforts to provide evidence of the Holocaust. Their words are particularly relevant because these people actually witnessed the most harrowing aspect of World War II, the extermination of six million Jews.

However, it is important not to forget that the massacre of the European Jews by the Nazis and their anti-Semitic European collaborators, took place in a systematic and industrial way in the middle of a full-scale war. A world war, and war in general, encourages countries, and therefore people, to carry out atrocities. This also happened during World War I, when the genocide of the Armenians and of Christians in the areas belonging to the Ottoman Empire, was carried out in order to accomplish the ethnic cleansing of a minority that was considered dangerous for the Turkish-Muslim identity[14].

The memory of the Holocaust has conveyed to the younger generations the horrors of war, anti-Semitism, the Nazi regime and fascism, the horrors of the Croatian Ustashas, the Hungarian Arrow Cross Party, the Romanian Legionaries, the Slovak Populists, and also of the other collaborators, mainly of Eastern Europe, involved in the Ukrainian or Baltic massacres.

I remember the impact that the Eichmann trial had in revealing the Holocaust to public opinion. I was eleven years old, and it was the first time I came into contact with real horrors of the war, the extermination of the Jews. These were facts and not just what families remembered. The memory of the Holocaust had a decisive function in developing our repulsion for war and in showing us its most despicable side. During the Cold War, despite the risk of war and the threat of

---

14. Cf. Andrea Riccardi, *La strage dei Cristiani: Mardin, gli armeni e la fine di un mondo* (Roma-Bari: GLF Editori, 2015).

a nuclear bomb, it was clear to most people that if humanity was to survive, keeping peace was the priority.

This awareness has gradually waned. With fewer and fewer witnesses of World War II left, people are once more considering war as an instrument for resolving conflicts and for asserting their own interests. In Afghanistan, Iraq, and Libya, despite the negative effects of military intervention, we have seen war justified as an instrument of international politics. For that matter, after 1945, for us Europeans war was something that concerned other people, except for the war in the Balkans. We enjoyed great peace but paradoxically, we gradually lost awareness of a policy of peace. The prevailing image became one of a technological war, almost "clean," basically a game, far removed from the "dirty war" in the trenches during World War I, or in Vietnam. The British Prince Harry wrote in his book *Spare*, that he remembered killing, from his Apache helicopter in Afghanistan, twenty-five people whom he considered pieces on a chess board.

The Legacy of War

It is worth going back to the insights on World War II, the result of meditating on the brutality of the war, which still provide decisive indications. These insights formed thought and the law and changed people's consciousness. The introduction to the 1945 Charter of the United Nations contains a mission, "to save succeeding generations from the scourge of war, which twice in our lifetime has brought untold sorrow to mankind." It goes on to say, "to ensure, by the acceptance of principles and the institution of methods, that armed force shall not be used, save in the common interest." The diminished international relevance of the United Nations is also the result of a reduced perception of the ideals proclaimed in the 1945 Charter.

From the UN Charter, it is a small step to the International Court of Justice in The Hague, established in 2002, and which, according to Habermas, "revolutionized international law... This revolution was born from the shock of the violent excesses of war."[15] It was based on the Rome Statute, which was signed at the height of globalization, when people optimistically believed that the unification of the markets would lead to a widespread increase in democracy and peace.

The legacy of war urged people to be wary of the risks of war. It was considered necessary to include this memory in the postwar constitutions and to define the *jus ad bellum*. This was the case for the introduction of the Constitution of the Fourth French Republic, and it was maintained in the Fifth one: France "shall undertake no war aimed at conquest, nor shall it ever employ force against the freedom of any people."

The French text influenced our Constitution to the extent that Giuseppe Dossetti was inspired by it in his proposal to the Constituent Assembly.[16] Palmiro Togliatti, in his speech on December 3, 1946, talked about "opposition... to the war that has ruined the country." Hence the idea expressed by the verb "reject." Meuccio Ruini from Reggio Emilia specified that "It has a strong emphasis and in this way implies a definite rejection of war." This is how Article 11 came into being and it is still a decisive guideline in Italian government policy making: "Italy rejects war as an instrument of aggression against the freedom of other peoples and as a means for the settlement of international disputes. Italy agrees on conditions of equality with other States, to the limitations of sovereignty that may be necessary to a world order ensuring peace and justice among the Nations."

---

15. Habermas, *A Plea for Negotiations*.
16. Giuseppe Dossetti, *La ricerca costituente: 1945–1952*, ed. Alberto Melloni (Bologna: Il Mulino, 1994).

After 1989, this legacy found itself struggling with the complex globalization of the world and with simplistic optimism, and it was not readily acknowledged. It was almost as though one were living in another period of history, that of the new century. The message appeared to have less of an impact on young generations: looking at the endless stream of images of war from all over the world became a habit encouraged by social media, without us ever being affected by the suffering of the victims and the soldiers. Has war once again become an inevitable element of history and of our future?

War brings out the forces of evil, as can be seen by all the violence that goes with it. A man from biblical times will see the stormy sea as uncontrolled chaos. War is chaos, the worst forces are released, and the worst of men stand out. Anne Frank, who was hiding in Amsterdam while the hunt for Jews was increasing, wrote in her diary, "There's in people simply an urge to destroy, an urge to kill, to murder and rage, and until all mankind, without exception, undergoes a great change, wars will be waged, everything that has been built up, cultivated, and grown will be destroyed and disfigured, after which mankind will have to begin all over again."[17]

We cannot resign ourselves to a war that devastates a population and risks never ending. This is often a characteristic of the wars of today, the fact that they never end with a victory or a defeat. Moreover, as one of the great Western leaders, who is not a pacifist, once told me, a lot of money is a stake too. One cannot underestimate Pope Francis's insistence on limiting the economic interests that dominate the arms market. The longer a war lasts, the more difficult it is to find peace, it is almost like going into a tunnel and not being able to see the end of it. Talking about peace does not

---

17. Quoted from Harold Bloom, *A Scholarly Look at the Diary of Anne Frank* (Philadelphia: Chelsea House Publishers, 2010) 244.

mean surrendering to the attacker, but it means carefully considering the price of every war and keeping constantly present the aim of living in peace.

The Loss of Peace in Syria

The war in Ukraine started within a series of wars that shed blood on the beginning of this twenty-first century. One of them in particular is related to the war in Ukraine, and this is the war in Syria, which is still going on. For the last twelve years, the country has been a battlefield between President Assad's national forces, various kinds of rebels, the Turkish army, Kurdish forces, Iranians, the Lebanese Hezbollah, and fighters from extremist groups, including the Islamic State (ISIS): the Syrian civil war is also related to a series of external interventions, including Turkey, Russia, Saudi Arabia, the United States, and France.

The repression of the "Arab Spring" protests marked the beginning of this war, with the arrest and detention of thousands of people. Syrian prisons have been reported to be places of horror, humiliation, and torture. Sednaya prison for example, which is not far from the ancient Christian site of Maaloula, where people still speak Aramaic, the language Jesus spoke, has been proved to be a place of horror, torture, and executions without trials. One inmate, fortunately freed, said, "The whole time I was there I only heard silence."[18] A deadly silence reigns over Sednaya, but Amnesty International has been able to break it. One inmate, a university professor, said, "I very nearly went crazy." Between 2011 and 2015 alone, over thirteen thousand people were killed, most of

---

18. Eugenio Dacrema, Marta Serafini, and Federico Thoman, *Dentro l'inferno delle prigioni di Assad*, in https://reportage.corriere.it/ esteri/ 2016/ dentro-linferno-delle-prigioni-di-assad.

them hung. At least ninety thousand people have disappeared from the Syrian government's illegal detention centers, and their families know nothing of the fate of their loved ones.

This is the true face of the Syrian regime, which uses criminal systems to terrorize its people and keep them under the control of the Alawite minority, to which the head of state belongs. Najah Almukai, a Syrian artist, a prisoner of the regime, painted the horror of the prison; nude, humiliated bodies, various kinds of torture and torture instruments, hollow eyes, stricken with terror. The regime defends itself every possible way and, as of today, it does not intend to give up occupying most of Syria. The people are hostages of the regime, but also of a spiral of misery, imposed by the deterioration of the economy and by international sanctions imposed on the Damascus government. Around 90 percent of Syrians live below the poverty line.

There are reports that three hundred thousand people have died. For the last twelve years, Syria has been torn apart by the war. It is now a country of 18.5 million people. Around 6.5 million refugees have fled. Aleppo, a city with a thousand-year history of coexistence between Christians and Muslims, has been under siege for such a long time that it is now called the "mother of all battles": over thirty-one thousand people have died, whole neighborhoods have been destroyed and thousand-year-old monuments razed to the ground. Anyone traveling around the country today will only see ruins everywhere, made even worse by the earthquake in February 2023.

In 2015, the question of admitting Syrian refugees divided Europe as the countries in Eastern Europe were against admitting them. Millions of refugees were left in camps in Lebanon, Turkey, and Jordan. The German Chancellor Angela Merkel intervened in favor of admitting Syrians with an expression that became famous—*Wir schaffen das.*

("We can handle this.") It was a brave gesture and Germany understood that it was a necessary decision, which also turned out to be beneficial for the German market. Eastern Europe however, gradually consolidated its decision not to accept refugees, particularly those coming from the Arab or Muslim world. This policy was motivated by the fear of Europe turning into a Muslim continent, which was thought would happen as a result of the refugees' ethnicities and religion "replacing" the existing ones.

In Hungary, this policy was accompanied by an economic commitment to some Middle East Christian communities, although the question of the presence of Christians in the Arab world is not at all of an economic nature. For example, in 2003, before the intervention against Saddam Hussein, there were 1.4 million Christians in Iraq, that is 6 percent of the population. Now there are less than three hundred thousand Christians, less than 1 percent of the inhabitants, because of the insecurity, internal struggles, and above all because of ISIS. The Western policy badly compromised the Christians' situation in Iraq. In Syria, the Christians used to account for around 10 percent of the population but now there are less than half that figure, only around 3 percent of the population.

The terrible earthquake in February 2023 that hit northern Syria and western Turkey attracted international attention and, because of the emergency, the sanctions were suspended. Refugees in the north of Syria were caught in the earthquake, as well as people living in Aleppo, which had already been through wars, sieges, and terrorism. In Syria and Turkey, twenty-four million people were reported to have suffered, a quarter of whom were children.

The political situation in Syria has been at a stalemate for years and there seems to be no solution to this ongoing war. This war has not led to peace at all, not even an unjust peace but with a halt to the fighting; on the contrary, it has become an everlasting war. This situation makes it possible for Turkey to extend its area of influence. At the same time, it makes it possible for those in power in Damascus to run what is left of Syria. Many children have grown up without experiencing even one day of peace.

The war in Syrian preceded and prepared the way for the war in Ukraine because of the way Russians fought, once they became involved—a brutal full-scale war without sparing civilians or buildings. It is obvious that Russia did not intend to lose that area, in which it could exert its influence, and aimed to confirm its standing as an empire. The man who led the operations is the Russian Commander Alexander Dvornikov, called the "butcher of Syria." He was sent to Ukraine at the beginning of 2022. The same methods the Russians adopted to wage war in Syria are being used in Ukraine. We could have noticed this unprecedented cruelty earlier, but at the time it did not seem to interest people very much, simply because it was happening in Syria. However, no war can really be considered far away because by now no population is isolated and everyone has access to information.

After Moscow's temporary loss of Libya with the fall of Ghaddafi, Russia became convinced that it could not lose Syria. It was its last stronghold on the Mediterranean Sea, and it could not risk completely losing its power in this area. Hence their stubborn desire to fight in Syria alongside Assad, Moscow's longtime ally since the days of President Hafez al-Assad and the Soviet Union. The war in Syria has also shown us that Europe does not count in such a critical context, especially considering the gradual withdrawal of the United States. Ten years earlier, there were demonstrations against the war in Iraq (in particular, against American intervention), but as far as Syria was concerned (although the players were different) European public opinion appeared to be disinterested and inert, even though it is now clear that the Iraq war prepared the way for the war in Syria.

The Destruction of a World

Faced with wars, in Ukraine but also in Syria, people talk about reconstruction; they may say, the resources for rebuilding these countries are already available. Maybe it is true, but still there is no peace. Moreover, even if there was the long-hoped-for peace, and therefore the possibility to rebuild, it is important to pay great attention to one fact: the reconstruction of a country, after such a far-reaching war, does not mean that the country will be resurrected. Something, perhaps a lot, has died forever in a country in which there has been a lot of fighting. The people who left the country may not come back, families have been split up, their children have grown up abroad.

Reconstruction is not only a question of healing war wounds. Something has ended forever and many scars will remain. Reconstruction can easily lead to uncontrolled building developments in towns and cities, a phenomenon that tends to go together with corruption when vast sums of money are involved. A country whose buildings have almost all been destroyed, that has lost its historical roots, and has suffered the displacement of its population, loses its identity and becomes susceptible to all kinds of easy colonization.

Our idea of reconstruction is too close to that of World War II and to the experience of Italy and Germany. First of all, Italy was not so badly destroyed as Germany, and although rebuilding Italy was a serious matter, it was only relatively so. Here, politicians involved in the reconstruction knew what they were doing because they had been active in the Resistance. The Allies were deeply committed both politically and economically, and the Italian politicians they dealt with were able to manage the reconstruction of the country.

In Iraq for example, whole worlds disappeared in the war. The coexistence of Muslims with Christians and other religious minorities, which were part of Mesopotamia's thousand years of history, was badly damaged. The political situation became polarized by the conflict between the Shiite majority and the Sunnis. So, back to Syria, will it be possible to rebuild Aleppo, the second biggest city in the country, as a place where Christians and Muslims can live together again?

I talked about Aleppo in 2017 in a small book called *La forza disarmata della pace* (*The Unarmed Power of Peace*), because for me this city is a symbol of the coexistence between Islam and minorities in the Arab world.[19] At that time, there were three hundred thousand Christians in a population of less than two million people. Already in 2014, I had launched an appeal, *Save Aleppo*, to create an "open city" that would save its population and its monuments: there had to be places where people could take a break from war and destruction. However, radical Muslims did not like Aleppo because it was gentle and liberal; a city, with its history and people of different ethnicities and religions, in which everyone could live together. Aleppo was once the crossroads of the Silk Road that linked Asia with the Mediterranean, Ancient archaeological findings prove that people have lived there for over ten thousand years. Abraham is said to have rested in the area during his wanderings.

The mosaic made up of the different populations was reflected in Aleppo's urban planning and in its architecture. The minaret of the Umayyad Mosque, erected in 1090, reminded people of the city's Islamic history; it had invited

---

19. Andrea Riccardi, *La forza disarmata della pace: movimento, pensiero, cultura* (Milan: Jaca Book, 2017), 41ff.

the people of Aleppo to prayer for nearly one thousand years but was destroyed during the war. It meant everything to the Arab Muslims. In Aleppo there were Christians, among others, Armenians; some of them had escaped the Ottoman persecution during World War I: Kurds, Circassians, Turks, Jews... Even under Assad's sharp-eyed regime, people lived together in harmony, in the mixed cultural context that was typical of Aleppo. In 2015, the Israeli security service evacuated the last Jewish family, the remainder of an old community that had safeguarded the Masoretic text of the Bible written before the year 1,000 AD. The so-called *Aleppo Codex*, read and commented on by Maimonides, is now kept in Jerusalem, where I was able to see it.

Just as monuments that have been destroyed cannot come back, neither is it possible to rebuild a lost culture of coexistence. The various religious and ethnic groups have adopted different strategies to survive, but there is fear and distrust everywhere and the weakest only want to escape.

Yesterday's world can never be rebuilt; Iraq, and Bagdad in particular, is an example of a pointless, destructive war that Barack Obama called a "stupid war." "Iraq twenty years later: homesickness, bribes and boat on the Tigris" is the headline of an article in the newspaper *Corriere della Sera*, by a journalist who traveled to Iraq and saw the rampant corruption behind the rebuilding of the country after the United States' attacks.[20] The Chaldean Patriarch Raphaël Sako spoke in an interview about the construction of a "sectarian system," on a religious basis: "Corruption cre-

---

20. Andrea Nicastro, "Iraq vent'anni dopo: nostalgia, mazzette e barche sul Tigri," www.corriere.it, March 19, 2023.

ated by the system destroys us. Everything that belongs to the state is stolen."[21]

In Mesopotamia, once the cradle of civilization, everything that belongs to its history and its memory has been suffocated by rebuilding, mainly uncontrolled building developments brought about by corruption. All that is left is the Iraqi National Museum, founded in 1926 by the British expert in Middle Eastern studies, Gertrude Bell, but raided in 2003. There, one still has the feeling that Iraq's roots are deeply immersed in history. Looking at the city of Bagdad, one can see that the past has been canceled, smothered in the traffic that follows no rules. One forgets that for years the city, which was founded in the second half of the eighth century, was an architectural jewel. The new Bagdad, in its urban planning, expresses the reality of its newly reconstructed society of whom 3 percent are ultra-rich people, all of them connected to politics, 12 percent are state employees, and the rest are poor workers.

In many parts of the world, even in historical cities, uncontrolled and speculative building is creating a new urban habitat with no roots and no soul. The destruction caused by war accelerates this process. Giovanna Locatelli, in *L'oro della Turchia* (*Turkish Gold*) highlighted how the uncontrolled urbanization, promoted by Erdoğan and his supporters, has disrupted the social fabric of whole districts of Istanbul and of other Anatolian towns and cities.[22] In the areas in Anatolia that were hit by the earthquake, it was clear that the extreme fragility of the buildings was the

---

21. Niccolò Magnani, "Il cardinal Sako a 20 anni dall'invasione Usa in Iraq: 'la corruzione divora tutto,'" in www.ilsussidiario.net, March 19, 2023.
22. Giovanna Loccatelli, *L'oro della Turchia. Il business dell'edilizia che ha stravolto l'aspetto del paese e il suo tessuto sociale* (Turin: Rosenberg & Sellier, 2020).

result of poorly regulated building developments. However, this is not so much about the war as it is about building new global towns and cities, in particular outside Europe, areas with no center, but vast peripheral agglomerations, and also the occasional gated towns, where there is the total separation of the rich from the poor. This comparison makes one think about how different European cities are, despite their limitations and their governments' speculative policies.

The war is also uprooting Ukraine's history. There is talk of thefts by Russians from Ukrainian museums in areas under Russian control, many works of art, churches, historical buildings, and monuments have been hit. Then, but this is another matter, there is the uprooting of millions of people, in particular children and young people. The longer the war lasts, the worse these wounds become. As mentioned above, the history of Ukraine in the twentieth century was marked by massacres and the uprooting of the population.

The Drama of Ukraine

These considerations bring us back to the drama of Ukraine, a great test of international responsibility today. We look at it in the double perspective of the freedom of an independent country, but also of people who are suffering and lives that have been lost. This war, within the series of other recent wars, stands out because of the coordinated involvement of the West, with military and political support for Kiev, but also because of the stalemate on the battlefield. The West will not let Russia win but the Ukrainians cannot risk an indefinite war.

Domenico Quirico, a war journalist, said, "After 2003, it is no longer possible to give a chronological limit to wars, to establish a beginning with its declaration and the end with the victory and the submission of the defeated side."[23] Is it a case of endless wars or wars that, like in Iraq, become endemic? The nature of war has changed, and as Quirico concludes, "If peace was once the purpose of war," by now "war has become the purpose of peace."

The endless nature of war can now be seen in Ukraine, at the expense of its people. There is also the fear of Russian expansionism going beyond Ukraine to the Baltic countries, other northern countries, and Moldavia. The strategy of the Kremlin, in fact, is a combination of being opaque and murky but at the same time brutally open. In his speech at the conference in Munich in 2007, Putin accused the world of being dominated by the United States and announced Russia's intention to reassert its own power. Unfortunately, the West, perhaps still exuberant with its own power, did not get the message. The Ukrainian conflict could also develop in another way. Some people think it is possible to overthrow Putin's regime. This would be a step that was taken in Iraq and in Libya, when a dictator was overthrown without there being a clear plan for a new regime and different leaders. However, most people in the West do not yet think in terms of overthrowing Putin, and in any case, it is not something Ukraine can do so far.

Morin said, "It is unlikely that Russia could occupy all of Ukraine or that Ukraine could invade Russia." [24] These are not just the words of an important and elderly man worried about peace. Mark Milley, the Chief of Staff (who retired, on September 30, 2023) of the United States, the country that is offering Ukraine the greatest support, said that the Russians are not able to overpower the Ukrainians, just as

---

23. Domenico Quirico, "Iraq, 20 anni senza un perché," in www.lastampa.it/esteri, March 20, 2023.
24. Morin, *Di guerra in guerra*.

it is very unlikely that in 2023 the Ukrainians will be able to recover the areas they have lost.[25] The stalemate seems to be permanent. Besides, even though Kiev can continue counting on Western support, Russia has shown remarkable resilience, despite sanctions, which it is managing to by-pass. The Chinese position is still uncertain, as are the effects of the Chinese peace talks initiatives. Everything points to the continuation of the war, with no winners and no losers, and the Ukrainians, as I have already said, will continue to pay the price.

In October 2022, during the interfaith meeting "The cry for peace," sponsored by the Community of Sant'Egidio in Rome, President Emmanuel Macron said, "It is a strange moment to talk about peace."

So, when, if not now? The right time never seems to come. The meaning of the word peace has been lost, and it has now become synonymous with the inability to deal with invaders (how is it possible to have anything to do with them in the face of the brutalities of an army of mercenaries?). There is no dialogue anymore and everything is entrusted to public statements and propaganda. Only a few threads still link Russia and the United States, and this is a very dangerous situation.

The brutality of war makes people lose touch with reality. What needs to be done today is to protect Ukraine's freedom but also to prevent the population from paying such a high price. It is necessary to combine these two requirements that today appear incompatible. The only way out of this complex situation is with diplomacy, in order to get the players to talk. So much has been invested in arms and military action but almost nothing in diplomacy and in considering an alter-

---

25. Giuseppe Sarcina, "Ucraina, il generale Usa Mark Milley: 'Nessuno può vincere la guerra,'" *Corriere della Sera*, February 17, 2023.

native vision of the future. A complex, contradictory world at war is at the same time hyper-connected and therefore cannot move forward without dialogue and without a vision concerning the public interest.

The Ukrainian population has the right to safe independence, but as Macron said, "one cannot change the map. Russia belongs to Europe. Therefore, peace in Europe is impossible unless the Russian question is resolved." Russia has an idea of its own security, related to the guarantee represented by a geographical belt that defends it. This idea, however, is no longer acceptable. Eastern Europe, which has only recently been liberated from the USSR, has a different perception than Western Europe, and it is afraid of Russia. This can be seen from the way Poland has armed itself. War can do nothing to bring these and other aspects together because it is manipulative, rigid, and ruthless.

Every war leaves a poisoned legacy. World War I set the stage for World War II, after which a large part of Europe found itself deprived of its freedom and controlled by the Soviet Union. This painful history of over forty years is precisely what is behind the anti-Russian attitude of many countries of Eastern Europe.

The Uprising against Being Irrelevant

What can we do? What can an ordinary citizen do when faced with decisions regarding war and international dynamics? Our lives are often dominated by a sense of helplessness. We are irrelevant. All we can do is support decisions made by other people with logic and dynamics that we do not always understand.

The great show of solidarity toward Ukrainians at the beginning of the war was surprising. Possibly, it was a way of expressing a form of protest against that narcissistic dictatorship of the ego that seems to make up the anthropologic substrate of our society. Actually, a similar openness manifested itself during the pandemic. Due to the cult of the ego, many ways of living together were abandoned a long time ago. This is how an Italian writer, Sebastiano Vassalli, describes the world today: "The present is a noise, billions, billions, billions of voices that shout together in all languages trying to drown out each other using the word me, me, me."[26]

We live in a world of "me," made up of selfishness, but also of loneliness and sadness. This "me" destroys the "us" of the family, the community, the Church. In this "me" there is also a lot of aggression. People who are alone feel irrelevant, they experience the effects of history without questioning them. It is difficult to think there can be a different approach to history. A great sage, the Othodox Archbishop of Albania said, "The opposite of peace is not war but egocentricity." Yes, social conflicts start from an exaggeration of the ego, but so do national conflicts. Basically, what is nationalism if not also a form of collective self-centeredness?

War is like the thief in the night that the Gospel talks about: it comes suddenly. Ukraine had been threatened for a long time but one day the country woke up to discover it had been invaded and the war had started. Stefan Zweig, a Jewish writer, whose books were burned by Hitler, committed suicide out of despair in 1940. He described the feeling of helplessness that overcame him when his country became involved in the war: "Just like the others, I stood in my room, as defenseless as a fly, as powerless as a snail, while my life and my death ... my future were at stake." When a war starts, a people's destiny is in the hands of the warlords.

---

26. Sebastiano Vassalli, *La chimera* (Turin: Einaudi, 1990), 3. Sebastiano Vassalli, *The Chimera* (London: Harvill, 1993).

Ukraine, as a wounded country, prompted people's solidarity. In every act of solidarity lies an action for peace. Solidarity counteracts the violence of the economy and an unjust society that makes more and more people poor. Solidarity has the ability to repair the torn fabric of society; it heals people of their loneliness and brings peace. The integration of foreigners is an act of peace because it prevents war and builds a society of people who live together. This is how the Ukrainian refugees were welcomed. International solidarity is an act of fraternity. It reduces distances and indifference with respect to other countries; it crosses borders and brings countries closer together. It is a political act that consolidates the awareness that we are one big family of nations who ultimately share a common destiny. In the long run, helplessness generates indifference that in turn creates laziness and fear, but also makes it possible for governments to make decisions in which the people play no part.

The arrival of the Ukrainians fleeing their country, challenged the widely spread attitude toward non-European refugees. Over the last few years Sant'Egidio has opened humanitarian corridors for over six thousand people. By welcoming and helping the refugees integrate, we realized how this process enriches Italy, a country that is going through a demographic crisis and needs new workers. Moreover, in every event that involves integration, there lies a commitment to peace.

To know, be informed about and follow events, means to take part closely and not turn away. A lively and well-informed public opinion influences events and political intentions and decisions. Peace has to be put back in the center as the aim of every policy and even of war itself, above all in Ukraine.

We cannot resign ourselves to war, the source of all forms of poverty. It is not only Ukraine but also Syria that has no peace; there are the wars raging continuously in Ethiopia, the oldest independent country in Africa, where at the time of this writing, eight hundred thousand people have died in Tigray, but also the wars sparked by Islamist terrorism in Africa. We do not even know the full extent of current wars. Looking for peace, I say this again, is not a question of surrendering to the aggressor, but it means considering the price of every war and constantly setting the goal of restoring peace. To achieve this, a culture of peace has to be reawakened and there has to be a peace movement that can put this goal at the center of politics.

Many believers are convinced that prayer is also a form of protest against war. The American biblical scholar Walter Brueggemann wrote, "The Church is offered a place in the Council of the Lord where decisions are made. . . . Jesus shares with us God's secrets."[27] Believers can ask God for the end of war or for peace on earth. We know that God wants peace, that peace is what is good for all peoples. Karl Barth, the great Reformed Church theologian wrote, "God is not deaf; He listens; He takes action. He does not take action in the same manner if we pray or if we do not pray. It has an influence on God's actions, on the very existence of God. . . . Our prayers are fragile and pitiful. Despite this, what counts is not whether our prayers are strong, but that God listens to them."[28]

Giorgio La Pira, the mayor of Florence who made his city the heart of the dialogue during the Cold War years said, "I believe in the historical power of prayer." He also invited the poor to join the prayers for peace in the Floren-

---

27. Walter Brueggemann, *Pace* (Turin: Claudiana, 2012), 156. Walter Brueggeman, *Peace* (St. Louis, Missouri: Chalice Press, 2001).
28. Karl Barth, *La preghiera: Commento al Padre nostro* (Turin: Claudiana, 2013), 28–29.

tine Badia. La Pira is a prototype of a Christian who fights for peace: he used to hold the Bible; he drew inspiration for peace from it and looked at the geography of nations and at their suffering.

Solidarity, prayer, and responsible participation are how unarmed people and pacifists "attack" war, and this is at the heart of their action for achieving peace. Making peace involves repairing the division between populations and between individuals and healing the wounds that war causes. However, war begins before the hostilities, when there is still the possibility to act so as to avoid the clash. This is preventive peace, the peace that prevents war. Deep divisions between people are caused by hate and the absence of dialogue. The first letter of John says, "All who hate a brother or sister are murderers" (1 John 3:15).

A Vision of Peace

It is necessary to resurrect a culture of peace that takes into account reality. Macron, in his speech quoted above said, "Peace is impure, deeply and ontologically, since it accepts a number of instabilities and discomforts that enable this coexistence between me and the other." This is reality. Peace requires vision, which today is lacking. Faced with the foggy horizon of war, we are unable to go any further. It seems that war alone is dominating the present; it is as though there cannot be peace, even with a victory. What is war anyway? Pope Francis expressed the wisdom of the Church (which Pope Paul VI defined as an "expert in humanity," in his speech at the UN in 1965), when he wrote, in the encyclical *Fratelli tutti*, "Every war leaves our world worse than it was before. War is a failure of politics and of humanity, a shameful capitulation, a stinging defeat before the forces of evil. Let us not remain mired in theoretical discussions but touch the wounded flesh of the victims."[29]

These few lines contain the wisdom developed during the wars of the twentieth century and, above all during the two World Wars, by the Church, a great supranational organization of the people. The Church is convinced that wars do not improve humanity, but they are its downfall. In a decidedly antiheroic tone of voice, Pope Francis does not exalt war as the way to victory, but says it is a "shameful surrender" to the forces of evil, war being "a defeat of politics." According to him, this is what we are experiencing because of the crises of diplomacy and political initiative. In his encyclical on peace, *Fratelli tutti*, the Pope invites us to understand once again what war is, starting by having direct contact with those who suffer [from war]; this is the only way to understand its reality. The avoidance of a direct relationship with so many war refugees, in fact, the rejection of them, has made us blind to the drama of war.

War dehumanizes everyone, even those who fight for just reasons. Simone Weil, who was critical of some aspects of pacifism, said that, starting with the war in Spain, every war dehumanizes those who fight in it: "One leaves as a volunteer, with the idea of sacrifice, and ends up in a war resembling a war of mercenaries but much crueler."[30] War inevitably transforms the nature of those who fight in it. Is it utopian to think of life beyond war?

In 1992, in an introduction to Emmanuel Kant's essay, *Perpetual Peace*, which was first published in 1795, Norberto Bobbio writes that, although more than two hundred years have passed, "It is the starting point for discussion and

---

29. Francis, *Fratelli tutti*, no. 261.
30. Simone Weil, *Sulla guerra. Scritti 1933–1943*, ed. Donatella Zazzi (Milan: Net, 2005), 53.

the guidelines for whoever is convinced that the problem of eradicating war is the crucial problem of our time."[31] Eradicating war is essential in a period in which it is being reassessed. We citizens are blocked by the political stalemate of the government. Blocked means being dragged down by the narrow-minded logic of those who fight against each other; they are forced to give up on any political direction and have no alternative vision of the future.

In 1932, Albert Einstein and Sigmund Freud wrote to each other about a question Einstein asked (the publication of their correspondence was forbidden in Nazi Germany), "Is there any way of delivering mankind from the menace of war?"[32] Einstein wrote, "Man has within him a lust for hatred and destruction, manipulated by those in power: an enigma that only the expert in the lore of human instincts can resolve." This is why he turned to the father of psychoanalysis. Freud accepted the challenge and acknowledged that the drive to hate and destruction is ready to welcome the "instigation" to fight. What is war for the father of psychoanalysis? "War destroys lives that were full of promise; it forces the individual into situations that shame his manhood, obliging him to murder fellow men, against his will; it ravages material amenities...."

War is inhuman and barbaric. According to Freud, *civilized development* will be able to end war. What does that mean and when will there be an end to this continuous story? Maybe it is a question of "mills that grind so slowly that, before the flour is ready, men are dead of hunger." He added that "a well-founded dread of the effects of future wars" may

---

31. Immanuel Kant, *Per la pace perpetua* (Rome: Editori Riuniti, 1992), XXIX.
32. Sigmund Freud, Albert Einstein, *Perché la guerra* (Bollati Boringhieri: Turin 2021) 59. https://en.unesco.org/courier/may-1985/why-war-letter-albert-einstein-sigmund-freud.

accelerate the end of wars. It is not cowardly to fear war. On the contrary, fear of war can lead to wiser decisions. In 1933, Einstein was touring the United States and decided to stay there because of Hitler's rise to power in Germany. Freud's works were banned in Germany that year, and in 1938 he left Austria, which was under Nazi control, and moved to London where he lived for a year until his death.

Eradicating war is the vision of the future, but how is this possible while a war is still going on? The father of psychoanalysis and the great physicist discussed it at length and in fact this question has been studied at least since the end of World War I. It seems strange that in the twenty-first century, war has been rehabilitated, in theory, and has by now become a common phenomenon. In the end, the aim to eradicate war seems to be relegated to the realm of utopias.

In 1946, Luigi Sturzo, who had not yet returned from exile in the United States, said, "War today has achieved such a technical and political scope that it has become an instrument out of proportion with the defense of any justified right…" He concluded, thinking about the changes that until then had been considered impossible: "We need to have faith that from today's chaos a new international order will arise, such that war, as an instrument to safeguard legal rights, will be abolished, as were polygamy, slavery, serfdom, and family vendettas."[33] It sounds impossible, but things can change.

After two decades during which war ended up being considered acceptable, one month after the invasion of Ukraine, Pope Francis spoke along the same lines and talked about the dream of the end of war in the history of humanity: "It is necessary to renounce the war in which fathers and mothers bury their sons, men kill their brothers whom they had

---

33. Luigi Sturzo, *Nationalism and Internationalism* (New York: Roy Publishers, 2006), 215.

not even met before, where those in power decide and the poor die... War cannot be inevitable, we must not get used to war! In the face of the danger self-destruction, humanity will understand that the moment of ending all wars has come, a moment to wipe it out of the history of man before it wipes out man from history."

Although peace has been lost in Ukraine and in many other countries, the fact that we can still enjoy peace where we live means we can offer our solidarity. I believe war makes us think about peace again, because we do not want this fragile world to be destroyed by war, or that war will be what the next generations experience. Thinking about peace means raising a consciousness of peace, so that public opinion can be free and attentive, and not limited by simplified versions of the facts. Peace means not being dominated by war, with its ruthless logic that we are unable to stop. Peace cannot be lost for too long because of the responsibility we bear toward all the people who have been torn apart by war. In addition, we must not forget that in this globalized and interconnected world, everything is communicated and interconnected, including war and peace. Thinking and sharing different opinions about all of this is not a waste of time; it is a way to prepare for better times to come.

Two

Remembering Wars, the Hope for Peace

Remembering Wars

Remembering World War I, over one hundred years after it ended, is of fundamental importance for Europe. That war was the origin of many issues of today's world. Remembering it means, first of all, recalling its dreadful numbers: around nine million soldiers and between six and nine million civilians perished (whereas during World War II, more civilians died than soldiers). Then, as a consequence, there was the displacement of populations, the onset of mental diseases, the so-called "war neurosis," or "shell shock," and epidemics, including the Spanish flu. The overall estimates were thirty-seven million deaths, which made World War I one of the bloodiest wars in history.

The first genocide of the twentieth century took place during that war: the newly established Turkish government carried out the systematic slaughter of the Armenian population, which also involved several Christian Churches. The other genocides of the twentieth century are connected to that first one, for instance, the Holocaust. Hitler apparently said something very significant about the Armenian genocide, although not everyone is convinced that it is historically true. He was addressing his generals, who were perplexed about his plans for mass murder: "Who, after all, speaks today of the annihilation of the Armenians?"[34]

---

34. Marcello Flores, *Il genocidio degli Armeni* (Bologna: Il Mulino, 2006), 271.

Who does remember the Armenians and who remembers World War I, apart from people with a particular interest in these events? So little attention is paid to wars, and now the generation that lived through World War II is disappearing. They remembered how the roots of that war could be found in the flawed peace, following the victory of World War I in 1918. Pope John Paul II, whose father was a soldier, was born in 1920, just after World War I and the re-emergence of Poland as an independent country. He saw the horrors of World War II, the massacres of Jews and Poles, and felt it his duty to bear witness to the madness of war. He did this with great determination. He was close to the peace movements when the United States attacked Iraq, and he said, "The generation to which I belong experienced the horror of war, the concentration camps, persecution.... I myself am a witness to much pain and many trials, having seen these in the years of my youth. My priesthood, from its very beginning, was marked by the great sacrifice of countless men and women of my generation."[35]

Many of us have known people who lived through World War II, some even World War I, who have often told us about the horrors of the war. One of the letters from 1918 written by an Italian infantryman (the Italians at the time were working class, farmers, and often illiterate, so they had someone write their letters for them) gave the most heartbreaking and simple definition of war: "It is called war because you end up buried."[36] The survivors of wars, like the millions of war veterans, but also the tragic survivors of genocide, have testified that war means the death of the masses. I met a Jewish

---

35. John Paul II, Ecumenical Commemoration of the Witnesses to the Faith in the Twentieth Century, May 7, 2000. www.vatican.va.
36. A play on words in Italian that cannot be rendered in English: "Guerra" (war) and "terra" (earth).

woman from Rome, Settimia Spizzichino, who escaped the Holocaust, and at the end of her life she wondered in distress:

> What will happen when we will no longer be here? Will the shameful memory be lost? Even today terrible things take place: wars, massacres, ethnic cleansing.... Each of those events makes me relive my personal tragedy, brings back the memory of what happened. That is why, to prevent similar things from happening again, I continue to remember and to speak of it; also, so as not to forget those who did not return. For my mother, my sisters, my brother, my nephew. For my murdered friends and all who died in Auschwitz, Bergen-Bergen, and in the other concentration camps.... For all the years stolen, stolen from millions of men, women, and children.[37]

The question of memory remains essential. This is why it is so important to talk about the war that ended in 1918, and the peace of 1919, which are the origins of the processes that led to World War II.

A Period That Is Familiar with War

We are living in a time only too familiar with war, and this is very disturbing because it is as though the deep resistance to it, founded on the memories of the two World Wars, no longer exists.

The war in Syria has been going on since 2011, and the outcome, as of today, is millions of refugees living abroad, maybe five hundred thousand deaths, and many missing, or

---

37. Settimia Spizzichino, Isa Di Nepi Olper, *Gli anni rubati: le memorie di Settimia Spizzichino reduce dai Lager di Auschwitz e Bergen-Belsen* (Cava de' Tirreni: VII Ripartizione, Politiche per gli Anziani, Progetto "Radici in Piazza," 1996), 75.

prisoners of the government or of various armed movements. Some of the people who disappeared were dear friends, like the Syrian Archbishop of Aleppo, Mons. Ibrahim, whom I met in 1986, and a Jesuit, Paolo Dall'Oglio, from Rome like me. We have been indifferent to what was happening and have let the war devour Syria, a hostage of conflicting international interests. European public opinion has been disinterested, unable to exert pressure on its governments or organize demonstrations for this unfortunate country. The UN and other countries too, have failed Syria, a country of twenty-two million inhabitants, which is still being devastated by the war. I know about the refugees' suffering because the Community of Sant'Egidio—together with Italian and French Protestants, the Church of France, and other organizations—have opened humanitarian corridors so that thousands of the most vulnerable refugees could come to Europe. This is a unique experience and also an initiative that other European countries could adopt.

The siege of Aleppo, which lasted from July 2012 to December 2016, was a dramatic example of the effects of war: it destroyed a great patrimony of humanity and consumed a city that was a witness to the beauty of Christians and Muslims living together in the same historical and cultural context. Aleppo was so lovely and so gentle! The Syrian poet Adonis described it as a city of coexistence: "The Church is a symbol/the Mosque is a voice/Between the two, life in Aleppo circulates like in a garden." Many churches have been destroyed and most of the Christians have left the country: maybe a third of them are left. Many mosques have been hit, so was the historical souk, even the Seljuk minaret of the Umayyad Mosque with its thousand-year history was blown up. The terrible war game in Syria has wiped out a way of living peacefully together, achieved over centuries of culture.

Where is the peace movement that acted forcefully against the intervention in Iraq in 2003, which, according to the United States press, mobilized millions of people to represent the third world power? No peace demonstrations for Syria have been seen. Wars are imposed on public opinion, which is helpless, insensitive, and above all submissive—basically selfish. The crisis of the peace movement and of the culture of peace highlights people's increasing familiarity with war, a lack of resistance to the use of violence, and the use of violence as a way of ending war. This is a serious problem, and the question is, why have we become less sensitive to peace?

The predominant idea that other countries' wars have nothing to do with us and that wars that last a long time do not trigger dangerous processes, is not true. Syria is an example: in Eastern Europe, the reaction to Syrian refugees was negative, and this caused the breakup of solidarity in the European Union, even though the number of refugees required to be admitted was limited. It is an illusion to think that in the globalized age, other countries' wars do not involve their whole area and beyond. This is clear when it comes to terrorism. Letting wars continue infects entire regions, if not the whole world, as in the tragic consequences of the war between Israel and the Palestinians.

Familiarity with war is also dangerous because public opinion is so emotional. Dominique Moïsi talks about a "geopolitics of emotions."[38] Emotions demand a reaction. The emotion resulting from the use, not yet proved, of gas in Goutha, near Damascus, produced a strong reaction in the United States and among its allies. However, the situation

---

38. Dominique Moïsi, *Geopolitica delle emozioni: le culture della paura dell'umiliazione e della speranza stanno cambiando il mondo* (Milan: Garzanti, 2009).

in Syria remains unaltered because the country is still held captive by this war. Internet communication, the culture of immediacy and of the here and now, the proliferation of information, and the multitude of players involved, all drive people to face reality from an emotional point of view and encapsulate their reaction in the moment rather than to process their reaction.

Public opinion is prey to emotions and therefore to the media, which manipulates it. Forgetting the horrors of the two World Wars and losing the memory of the Holocaust means moving irresponsibly along the edge of war and endorsing the use of violence. We need our history and memories; it is impossible to experience the complexity of the global world without an awareness of history.

Why History Is Necessary

History is crucial for the collective memory because it delivers human events and war from the oblivion into which people often fall because they are obsessively preoccupied by the present and by themselves. History releases the memory of war from the typical self-celebration of victory and heroism, which in any case does not mean much today. In this period, history is becoming separate from politics and is in line with the media, which are decisive tools for obtaining and consolidating consensus and mobilizing emotions. History almost only exists as an academic subject. In a continent like Europe, permeated with history, it is difficult to live and govern without it. We are left oblivious to reality and blind when facing the future.

War needs to be historicized and remembered, otherwise it is like a ghost that hovers above the events of the world. I would like to mention an outstanding historian, Marc Bloch (the founder with Lucien Febyre, of Annales, the journal of social history), who was born in 1886. He was a non-practicing Jew who fought during World War I, first as a sergeant and then as a captain, and fought again in 1939 during World War II. Immediately after the end of World War II, Bloch felt the need to write about the two wars and his manuscripts were then published. He talked about life in the trenches: "It occurred to me that the faces of men who await death and fear it are not beautiful to look at...."[39] He wanted to use his notes for a history of World War II. In his book *Strange Defeat*, written in 1939–40, Bloch described the breakdown of the high-ranking French soldiers in the face of the German advance. He wrote:

> The worst was that this confusion happened to those who carried the heaviest responsibility. With horror, almost every day many of us noticed the frightening increase of suffering in some officials who occupied the most important positions as chiefs of staff.... The first symptoms were physical ... empty eyes, badly shaved, nervousness which, from feverish restlessness about irrelevant things, abruptly changed into a show of impossible serenity.[40]

These are details reporting what the historian, not himself a pacifist, saw. Bloch knew what it meant to defend France. He fought as a volunteer during World War II against the Nazis and then, when France was defeated, he joined the Resistance. He was arrested, tortured, and shot by the Gestapo in 1944. As a historian and a fighter, Marc Bloch teaches us a great civic lesson: he reminds the world of culture

---

39. Marc Bloch, *La guerra e le false notizie: ricordi (1914–1915) e riflessioni (1921)* (Rome: Donzelli Editore, 2004), 16.
40. Marc Bloch, *Strange Defeat: A Statement of Evidence Written in 1940* (New York: Octagon Books, 1968).

and politics of their duty to keep historical memory alive, especially that of war.

Even in extreme situations, like in the concentration camps or in the Jewish ghettos during the war, where the determination to survive was being suffocated, there was still the need to leave a historical memory. Notes and descriptions of the hell experienced in Auschwitz were found in bottles and flasks during excavations carried out around the crematorium ovens. These were written by the Jews who were assigned to carry out work involved in the murders, called the Sonderkommando prisoners, who were then killed by the Nazis so they would not be able to provide proof of the massacres. Writing was an act of resistance to evil and an expression of trust in humanity, so that one day someone would listen to the voice of their grief. A note written by Salmen Gradowski on September 6, 1944, reads:

> I wish to leave this paper, just like many other notes, to be remembered by the new peaceful world, so that one would know what happened in this place. I have buried it under the ashes, believing it was the safest place, from where one day it will be dug up in order to find the memory of millions of people killed ... so the world can see at least a drop, a fragment of the tragic world we have live in.[41]

Memory aspires to be more powerful than death. Among the many expressions of this will to remember beyond all odds, I want to share the writings of a teenager, Abram Cytryn, a Jew who lived in the Lodz ghetto and who died in Auschwitz. He had the soul of a poet and here he explained why he started writing about this enclosure

---

41. Cf. *La voce dei sommersi: Manoscritti ritrovati di membri del Sonderkommando di Auschwitz*, ed. Carlo Saletti (Venice: Marsilio, 1999).

of sorrow: "Living in the hell of the ghetto and seeing the blood of my brothers flow, I decided to put on paper my testimony.... I would like their blood to splatter onto the paper to convey to future generations the memory of those ruthless years."[42]

The Globalized World

History takes us to the roots of what Eric Hobsbawn, a British historian, called the "Age of extremes: the short twentieth century."[43] He considered the twentieth century as the era of great cataclysms between two dates—1914, the beginning of World War I, and 1991, the end of the Cold War and the Soviet Union, created after the Russian revolution of 1917. This "short century" witnessed the globalization of war, first in 1914 and then in 1939. During the twentieth century, the wars among Europeans set fire to the world twice.

The Europeans fought against each other, also involving many non-European nations. Pope Benedict XV said that war would wear Europe out. The victors were not aware of this, as could be seen by their arrogance in 1919, when they believed they could rule the whole world. For example, with the end of the Ottoman Empire, the Middle East came under the control of Great Britain and France for just twenty years. Even the Crusaders' rule lasted much longer.

After 1945, Europe was no longer the power it used to be. Starting from India, Britain's largest colony, the jewel in its crown, the colonial empire with its countries that gave the map of the world the same color as their mother-

---

42. Abram Cytryn, *Racconti dal ghetto di Lodz: Gli scritti ritrovati di un adolescente morto ad Auschwitz*, ed. Frediano Sessi (Venice: Marsilio, 2016), 27.
43. Eric Hobsbawm, *The Age of Extremes: The Short Twentieth Century, 1914–1991* (New York: Viking Penguin, 1994).

land, continued its decline. This short century indicates the transition from the world dominated by Europe to a global and polycentric world in which, despite still being a prominent economic and cultural player, Europe is no longer its center.

Nowadays we find ourselves in a long period, moving toward the future without any grand vision or plan. Unlike in the twentieth century, the world has become broader, full of players, but no longer having one or more leaders. It is the world of globalization (the opening up of markets and the end of walls and borders) and of the reaction to it (the revival of national and religious identities and the consequent reinstatement of borders and walls). The global world therefore also involves processes of anti-globalization and post-globalization. In addition, it has, as it is important to repeat, a dangerous familiarity with war and violence unexpected at the end of the Cold War, in what was supposed to be the beginning of a time of peace.

Another characteristic of the global world is the widespread violence of mafias and criminals whose strategies aim to dominate with recurrent forms of terrorism that fuel the fear of our fellow citizens. There are so many, an infinite number of players in the global world: schooling, the media, and the Internet, that influence people's way of thinking. The Internet gives people the illusion that anything can be said in a debate. The world, with its millions of people, often expresses what Pankaj Mishra in "*The Age of Anger*"[44] called "resentment," because they do not have enough room for themselves or have a future. Resentment is a breeding ground for the culture of radicalization. In addition, Mishra wrote, "It poisons the civil society and ruins political freedom, and

---

44. Pankaj Mishra, *The Age of Anger: A History of the Present* (London: Allen Lane, 2017).

currently is preparing a global change bringing about toxic forms of chauvinism."[45]

In 1989 we would have never believed that democracies would find themselves in trouble, or imagined that war could be justified, whereas now we are seeing for ourselves the crisis that democracies are going through. It is complex, and when people are faced with complexity, they find simplistic solutions attractive: the Hungarian philosopher Ágnes Heller calls it "Bonapartism."[46] This is happening in Europe too now. It is the dangerous attraction for order understood as force: the contempt for democratic mechanisms and for a pluralism of ideas. There is currently widespread violence and crime in many countries in Asia, Latin America, and Africa. Democracy looks like a weakness, but it is not so. If there is a crisis among traditional political parties, then a grassroots political culture needs to be promoted. It must be able to involve as many citizens as possible, becoming the basis of the resilience of civil society. This is why it is necessary to invest in education, culture, and the study of history. Democracy is the only way different people can live together.

The Church, a Source of Humanity and Peace

In our global world, in which democracy and peace are not always undisputed values, we have two great resources of a different nature, consisting of a number of variables for facing a difficult future. These two solid guarantees for a more humane future are Europe and the Church.

---

45. Ibid., 17.
46. Danilo Taino, "Il bonapartismo è ancora qui. Intervista con Agnes Heller," *Corriere della sera* insert, "La lettura," 2016, 26–27.

In 1945, in the midst of the horrors of the concentration camp in Dachau, an Italian Dominican, Giuseppe Girotti, who was deported because he had been hiding Jews, preached before he died: "The Church used to be, and still is, the only shelter of the sense of humanity, love and mercy: sanctuary of truth, the principles of just reason, civility and culture."[47] This is the expression of the humanism of martyrs. It is a decisive element in the life of twentieth-century Christianity, which in this century has again created martyrs, as in the first centuries after the birth of Christ. The humanism of martyrs is a vision of reality: it is not elaborate but is vital and profound.

During the twentieth century, the Church, especially when faced with war, developed a consciousness that it owed the world a prophecy of peace, because it felt an inseparable connection with its aspirations for peace. There has been no lack of occasions on which the Church identified itself with countries and their defensive or offensive policies. In 1917, from the pulpit of Notre Dame, the French Dominican, Father Dalmace Sertillanges, argued with Pope Benedict XV, "Most Holy Father, we cannot, at the present moment, embrace your words of peace.... Our peace will not be a placatory peace. It will neither be, and we are really sorry, the peace of fatherly authority which will cover both sides: It will be peace through war...."[48] Even today these are words that could be spoken by religious figures.

It was in fact during World War I, above all thanks to Pope Benedict XV, that the Church's ministry of peace developed, even though hardly anyone took any notice of it, and it was even ridiculed. The Pope, as the head of the faith-

---

47. Giulio Malaguti, *Martirio di pace: Memoria e storia del martirio nel XVII centenario di Vitale e Agricola* (Bologna: Il Mulino, 2004).
48. Alberto Melloni, *Benedetto XV: Papa Giacomo Della Chiesa nel mondo dell'"inutile strage,"* Giovanni Cavagnini and Giulia Grossi, eds. (Bologna: Il Mulino, 2017), 353.

ful of all nations, felt that World War I was like an internal wound. Meanwhile, beyond nationalist logic and manipulations of propaganda, he saw catastrophic destruction. In an open letter of August 1, 1917, Pope Benedict XV wrote his famous phrase about war, which all his successors have fully shared: "A struggle which every day, even more, appears to be a useless massacre." War is a "useless massacre." The Church, with its experience in human nature, feels that war leaves the world worse than how it found it. In the letter of 1917, there is a farsighted observation regarding Europe: "Will the civilized world, therefore, be reduced to a field of death? And will Europe, so glorious and flourishing, almost overwhelmed by a universal madness, rush to the abyss, to its true and authentic suicide?"[49]

The Pope seems to testify to the common humanity that binds peoples and the horror of war that destroys it. One day Pope Benedict XV was with Achille Ratti, the future Pope Pius XI and he said:

> They want to silence me. The Representative of Christ should not have to summon peace. They will not succeed in sealing my lips. Woe if the Representative of the Prince of Peace was silent in the hour of the storm! The spiritual fatherhood invested in me makes it my duty to invite children from opposite sides of the barricade who are killing each other to make peace. I am and I feel that I am the spiritual Father of the soldiers of both sides. Nobody can stop the Pope from shouting to his own children: peace, peace, peace![50]

---

49. Benedetto XV, *Lettera ai Capi dei Popoli belligeranti*, August 1, 1917, in www.vatican.va. https://www.pas.va/en/magisterium/benedict-xv/1917-1-august.html
50. Ibid.

During a war, the Church is the place where the sense of humanity takes refuge. This is also the case today with respect to the serious problems that are afflicting nations, refugees, and immigrants. In the difficulties of this period, which is so emotional and constantly changing, its words represent important guidelines for preserving a sense of humanity. Experiencing the suffering caused by war strengthens our conviction that peace alone is holy, as Pope Francis and others have said. I would also like to mention the important words of a prominent Christian of the twentieth century, the Orthodox Patriarch of Constantinople Athenagoras, who was born in 1886, the same year as Marc Bloch, and who lived through World War I in the Balkans, in Macedonia:

> At Monastiri (today, Bitola, in Macedonia) I got to know Slavs well. I also observed the Germans and the Austrians. I lived with the French for two years. Every people is good. Everyone deserves respect and admiration. I have seen men suffer. Everybody needs love. If they are bad, maybe they have never encountered true love, which does not squander words, but irradiates light and life. I know dark forces, demons, exist, that sometimes take possession of men or nations, but the love of Christ is more powerful than hell. In his love we find the courage to love men and discover that, in order to exist, we need all men and all nations to exist as well.[51]

In this sense, Christianity is and will always be a great source of peace.

---

51. Athenagoras and Olivier Clément, *Umanesimo spiritual: Dialoghi tra oriente e occidente*, ed. Andrea Riccardi (Cinisello Balsamo, Milan: Edizione San Paolo, 2013), 82.

Europe

Countries in Europe, as I mentioned before, have the historical responsibility for having fought against each other in a war that became World War I. They have the responsibility, by the peace established in 1919, for having set the stage for World War II. In fact, even when wars are over, they leave a bitter legacy that poisons history. Two great empires disappeared in 1918, the Habsburg Empire and the Ottoman Empire, and with them centuries of coexistence of different peoples and religions. Only Russia was left, as an empire, but tragically transformed into the Soviet Union, with its ambition to build a new world.

War seemed to establish nations and nationalism as the most appropriate political reality for the world in the twentieth century. The Paris Peace Conference aimed to create the basis for ethnically homogenous countries and encourage their self-determination. This aim was only partially achieved because different populations had lived together in the same countries for centuries. The short century was one of nations whose minorities were often not acknowledged, and where anti-Semitism and nationalist totalitarianism were developing fast, the most tragic expression of which was Nazism. Between the two wars, the number of democracies decreased, whereas authoritarian and nationalist regimes, such as fascist regimes increased. Fascism in Italy introduced racial laws that discriminated against the Jews and declared the existence of a so-called Aryan race. Nobody objected.

Today the world, as we can see above all in towns and cities, is full of people of different ethnicities and religions who live together. There is no more ethnic-religious and national homogeneity. In emotional societies, the fear of people who are different increases. The global world seems to us to be invasive because of the migration flows that bring with them different ways of life. Should we protect ourselves more from others? The real problem is that too many people encourage resentment, instead of working on possible ways to live together. They do not realize that the process of integration guarantees a future on two levels, one national and one as part of the European Union.

European integration has been a guarantee of peace since it was first thought of by its founders, who all had, and I do not want to apologize for saying this, a Christian vision. European integration started, in my opinion, by considering Auschwitz as the extreme evil of World War II. The process of integration is the true guarantee of peace for Europe which, if it had more diplomatic and military resources, would also be a guarantee of peace for the whole world.

Men and women, children of the global world, are autonomous subjects in a world in which they often feel marginalized. This condition does not only concern immigrants in Europe but also Europeans themselves. They are often alone because the global world has dissolved so many social and political networks. Urbanization has created places where people live in solitude. Today the towns and cities in Europe are facing a great challenge in the attempt to live in peace. This involves social integration, dialogue, and the creation of communities in which people feel close to one another, as well as the development of popular cultures that help individuals to not feel disoriented, which can otherwise become dangerous.

Peace concerns the international political leadership, but also society, as a whole. What threatens peace also comes from society itself. We need to create a widespread culture of peace. Pope Francis, speaking about Europe, said, "Peace will be lasting in the measure that we arm our children with the weapons of dialogue, that we teach them to fight the good fight of encounter and negotiation. In this way, we will bequeath to them a culture capable of devising strategies of life, not death, and of inclusion, not exclusion."[52]

Peace will be lasting if we do not lose the historical memory of war, if the Church is a prophet of peace, if we are solidly integrated into Europe, if a fabric and culture of peace regenerate social life, and if we are able to arm ourselves with the weapons of dialogue to include everyone in both a small and big way. This is complex and it involves a lot of people and energy, which the simplifiers do not like because they prefer the so-called quick solutions of authoritarianism and wars, which, however, never end.

---

52. Francis, Conferral of the Charlemagne Prize. Address of His Holiness. May 6, 2016, in www.vatican.va. https://www.vatican.va/content/francesco/en/speeches/2016/may/documents/papa-francesco_20160506_premio-carlo-magno.html.

Three

The Culture of Hatred and Nationalism

Hatred Is Old, but Also Very Present Today

The history of hatred, like that of love, is the oldest of humanity. In the story of Cain and Abel, in the Bible, the book of Genesis says, "Cain attacked his brother Abel and killed him" (Gen 4:8). Hatred, as a culture, a feeling, a driver of action, is reflected in an infinite number of human affairs, experiences, and legends: it often explodes when people are in close contact with each other, like in the case of Cain and Abel, who were brothers, one a farmer, the other a shepherd. In fact, there is no history of hatred or of love when people are not close to each other, when they do not know each other, or when they live far apart: either there is mutual indifference, or they ignore each other.

Nonetheless, in today's world, an indifferent distance is often impossible. Liliana Segre warned us about the tragic role of indifference during the deportation of the Jews. She felt it herself when she left the railway station in Milan which was in German hands.[53] The Holocaust Memorial at the Milan station, from which she departed in 1944 with many other Jews toward what was supposed to be their final destination, symbolizes this. Indifference almost always becomes the decision to shirk from our responsibility because we know that this responsibility is toward others and what is happen-

---

53. Cf. Liliana Segre, *Sopravvissuta ad Auschwitz. Liliana Segre fra le ultime testimoni della Shoah*, ed. Emanuela. Zuccalà (Milan: Paoline, 2005).

ing to them. We think that our "salvation" will benefit by our distancing ourselves from them.

The effects of the global world, including the displacement of populations and the upheavals within social realities, bring together people who for centuries ignored each other because of their indifference or because of the physical distance between them. More and more, the alternatives that present themselves are either to live together or to hate each other and fight. Amy Chua, in a book she wrote a few years ago called *The World on Fire*,[54] points out how global capitalism encourages what she calls the age of hatred. According to Chua, capitalist globalization has unleashed a multiplication of violence and a real age of hatred.

There is, however, a particular type of hatred, present well before the global age, but still in existence and in fact really thriving. It is the culture of hatred related to the beginning and growth of the idea of a nation. A nation is a recent phenomenon in the long history of humanity. Nonetheless, to legitimize itself, it shows that it has always existed or at least existed before the others that also insist on having occupied the same or neighboring territory. Self-accreditation is part of the nation's narrative. In its representations, the nation becomes more and more like the homogenous house belonging to a population, even though its geography and demographics provide different results.[55]

Nationalism has organized and directed hatred, possibly only like religions but without that principle of internal contradiction that has changed and purified religions, which are more complex and stratified cultures. This can clearly

---

54. Amy Chua, *The World on Fire: How Exporting Free Market Democracy Breeds Ethnic Hatred and Global Instability* (New York: Anchor Books, 2004).
55. Cf. Ernest Gellner, *Nations and Nationalism* (Ithaca, New York: Cornell University Press, 1983).

be seen in the twentieth century. The Polish poet Wislawa Szymborska, who won the Nobel Prize for Literature, experienced the twentieth century in the painful perspective of Poland as a country that was torn apart, reborn and occupied. She wrote:

> Look how it is always efficient.
> How it keeps itself in form
> In our century of hatred.[56]

National culture has been a great container that has made hatred efficient, preserved it over the years and spread it like the development of an identity. History, language, geography, and literary epics have contributed to it. National culture (history, language, geography, epic literature) is obviously very important, but hatred lurks silently in its depths, and from time to time it explodes.

The Nation and Nationalism

Nothing seems more natural than a nation. It is almost like a physical characteristic that precedes and predetermines an individual. Yet the invention of the nation is part of contemporary history.[57] The invention (giving the word a significance of original creation) of nations goes back in different ways, to the nineteenth century, to the point of creating nationalism. With rare exceptions, this occupies the self-awareness of people and their relations with others. In France the history of the nation is long and diversified. It is older in Spain but still unresolved, as can be seen in the

---

56. Wislawa Szymborska, *La fine e l'inizio*, ed. Pietro Marchesani (Milan: Libri Scheiwiller, 2009), 33. The title of the poem is "L'odio" ("Hatred").
57. Cf., Eric J. Hobsbawm, and Terence O. Ranger, eds. *L'invenzione della tradizione* (Turin: Einaudi 2002).

Catalan question, a typically repressed population with its problem of autonomy and now of independence.

Nations that have been reinvented (it would be more acceptable to say "rediscovered") often have to free themselves from the rule of the states that repress their identity and aim to eliminate their national characteristics. In 1817, the Romantic philologist Vaclav Hanka "found" fragments of a manuscript, in the crypt of a church in a Bohemian village. It represented an extremely important national literary monument.[58] It was the beginning of the construction of a (forged) national poem that referred to a pure and just pre-Germanic age, that the Czech people could experience again. This happened partially with Czechoslovakia and definitively after the end of communism and the split from the Slovaks. These are the literary origins of nationalism.

From the beginning of the nineteenth century, the intellectuals were the promoters of the idea of the nation. People were proposed an identity that was different from the way they had always defined themselves, that is, by religion or at most by their region, especially during the past Habsburg and Ottoman Empires, which were multireligious and multiethnic.[59]

Even in the first decade of the twentieth century, an Anatolian peasant, a subject of the Ottoman Empire, who conceivably spoke Turkish, would have expressed his identity like this: "By the grace of God, I am a Muslim." A few

---

58. Cf. Jean Plumyène, *Le nazioni romantiche: Storia del nazionalismo nel XIX secolo* (Firenze: Sansoni, 1982), 149.
59. Cf. Tony Judt, Timothy Snyder, *Thinking the Twentieth Century* (New York: Penguin Press, 2012); Alan Sked, *The Decline and Fall of the Habsburg Empire, 1815–1918* ((London: Longman, 1989); Sean McMeekin, *The Ottoman Endgame: War, Revolution and the Making of the Modern Middle East, 1908-1923* (New York: Penguin Books, 2016).

decades later, thanks to the nationalization carried out by Atatürk, he would have said, "I am proud to be Turkish," and even today in the Anatolian mountains, it is still possible to see signs with the words "Proud to be Turkish." In fact, since the 1920s the Turkish national identity has spread to the point where Turkey is convinced it can assimilate the Kurds, who on the other hand, continue to resist, proclaim, and cultivate their own identity.[60]

The idea of a nation gradually moved away from the intellectuals and political elite to the people, in processes that George Mosse called the "nationalization of the masses."[61] These are different processes, which have taken place at various times, always building up the "us" as opposed to "them" or, in a particular and frequently hateful way, "the other." The Kurds, who fought with the Turks against the Christian Armenians at the beginning of the twentieth century, did not have the national awareness of being Kurdish, as do the Kurds today who are demanding their autonomy in the eastern areas of Turkey.[62]

The nationalization of the masses, especially in the twentieth century, was accompanied by propaganda aiming at making people feel they belonged, to the extent of introducing the notion of the religion of the fatherland. Fighting and dying in war for the nation required a great deal of convincing for men to enlist. The propaganda of the two world wars is one example: it was full of hatred on the part

---

60. A. Solaro, *Nazionalismo e Islam nostalgie imperiali ad Ankara*, in *ARES* (1995), Year III, nos. 6–7.
61. George L. Mosse, *The Nationalization of the Masses: Political Symbolism and Mass Movements in Germany from the Napoleonic Wars through the Third Reich* (New York: Howard Fertig, 1975), 1st ed. See also George L Mosse, *Masses and Man: Nationalist and Fascist Perceptions of Reality* (New York: Howard Fertig, 1980).
62. Cf. Andrea Riccardi, *La strage dei cristiani. Mardin, gli armeni e la fine di un mondo* (Roma-Bari: Laterza, 2015).

of the French for the Germans and vice versa, or of hatred for Austrians who occupied Italian areas, such as Trent and Trieste during World War I.

Words and language were crucial in this context. Images of the enemy's crimes started to circulate. Photographs showed the horrors of the war, and in response, in 1863, after Italian War of Independence, the Red Cross was set up.[63]

Nationalism and nationalization are multifaceted realities that contaminate and contradict each other. Many people, starting with Federico Chabod, the great historian of the twentieth century, have noticed that in Europe the processes of nationalization follow two models.[64] One is of French origin, the "daily plebiscite," as per Ernest Renan.[65] It is a cultural, voluntary, political, assimilatory model, so much so that Napoleon, a Corsican, could become emperor of France. The Italian model is similar and in fact Dalmatians in Trieste and Fiume, despite having Slavic surnames, speak and feel Italian. The other model, the German one, is based on "land and blood" and values lineage. In this case, the nation is a reality that people are born into but cannot become a part of and neither can they easily leave it. This model became the one of the Slavic people as well.[66]

Every nation has its enemy. At the beginning of the nineteenth century, liberal Europe was enthusiastic about

---

63. Cf. François Bugnion, *The International Committee of the Red Cross and the Protection of War Victims* (Geneva: International Committee of the Red Cross, 2012).
64. Federico Chabod, *L'idea di nazione* (Bari: Laterza, 1972).
65. Cf. Ernest Renan, *Qu'est-ce qu'une Nation?* text of a conference delivered at the Sorbonne on March 11, 1882 (Paris: Presses-Pocket, 1992). See Columbia Studies in Political Thought/Political History series, *Ernest Renan, What is a Nation? and Other Political Writings*, translated and edited by M.F.N. Giglioli (New York: Columbia University Press, 2018).
66. Cf. Nicolao Merker, *Il sangue e la terra: Due secoli di idee sulla nazione* (Rome: Editori Riuniti, 2001).

supporting Greece, and young volunteers, like the English poet Byron, set off to take part in the war to liberate Greece from the Turks, to fight the "abhorrent crescent" and, as Byron put it, the "dark flock, crowd enslaved to the sabre." It fueled the fear of the Turks.[67] With the independence of Greece, all traces of the Turkish-Muslim presence in the country were removed, including the mosques and minarets, even centuries-old ones, and the panorama became what we see today. The antagonism between the Greeks and the Turks continued during World War I, followed by the end of the Ottoman Empire, the burning down of Smyrna, the pogrom against the Greeks of Istanbul in 1955, the war between Greeks and Turks in Cyprus, where Nicosia was the last European city divided by an ethnic and religious wall into Greek and Turkish Cypriots.[68]

The Nationalization of Cities

Some cities have been deeply affected by national hatred which has radically changed them. A symbol of Greek-Turkish hatred is Thessaloniki, now the second largest city in Greece.[69] During the early twentieth century it was part of the Ottoman Empire. This is where Atatürk, the founding father of the new Turkey, was born (the Turkish government turned the house where he was born into a museum). For centuries, the city had been a world of coexistence between Turkish and Balkan Muslims, Orthodox Greeks, and Jews. After 1912, Thessaloniki became Greek and soon transformed its urban and ethnic physiognomy. In 1917, a vast fire destroyed the

---

67. Cf. Plumyène, *Le nazioni romantiche*, 193ff.
68. Vincenzo Greco, *Greci e turchi tra convivenza e scontro: Le relazioni greco-turche e la questione cipriota* (Milan: Franco Angeli, 2007).
69. Mark Mazower, *Salonica, City of Ghosts: Christians, Muslims, and Jews, 1430–1950* (London: Harper Collins, 2004).

Ottoman district. Most of the people who lived there were Muslims who afterward fled to Turkey. Many Jews left, too. The last Jews in the city were the ones deported by the Nazis during World War II. The Jewish community had been such an integral part of the city that when Thessaloniki was under Ottoman rule, the day of rest for the week there was Shabbat. The nationalism of the twentieth century greatly altered the cultural and urban features of the old Turkish-Greek-Jewish Thessaloniki and turned it into the second largest Greek city.[70] Mark Mazower, a historian, appropriately called his book on the city, *Salonica, City of Ghosts*.[71]

Important changes have often taken place in cities in Europe, particularly where the inhabitants are of different ethnicities and where, even though they have lived together for centuries, nationalistic hatred is behind a deep reshaping of urban identity. Thinking about Raul Pupo's studies, I remember Fiume, an Italian town with its Slavic hinterland, where even families with Slavic names spoke Italian. It became Croatian when it was made part of Yugoslavia. Fiume went through the assimilation imposed on it by the fascists, the Holocaust and the Foibe massacres of the Italians.[72] These were complex, cosmopolitan urban worlds, a cross between different ethnic universes, impractical in the Europe of nations.

Lviv was like that too. It was called Lwow in Polish, Lviv in Ukrainian, Lvov in Russian and Lemberg in German and Yiddish. Lviv used to be part of the Habsburg Empire but after 1918, it became Polish. In 1939, as a result of the Molotov-Ribbentrop Pact, Lviv became part of the Soviet Union. It was occupied by the Germans in 1941, and in 1945,

---

70. Cf. Gilles Veinstein, *Salonique, 1850–1918: La ville des Juifs et le réveil des Balkans* (Paris: Editions Autrement, 1992).
71. Mazower, *Salonica, City of Ghosts*.
72. Cf. Raoul Pupo, *Fiume. Città di passione* (Rome-Bari: Laterza, 2018).

it found itself once again in the Soviet Union. It has been part of independent Ukraine since 1991. This is a city that has gone through various sovereignties, all of which were marked by ethnic-national wars. Over half of its inhabitants were Polish, 30 percent were Jews, and the rest were Ukrainians. There was also an Armenian minority, of which only a beautiful church remains. In 1941, when it was occupied by the Germans, there were one hundred thousand Jews in the ghetto. Most of them were taken away and murdered. In July 1941, two pogroms were carried out (the second one was called Petjura Days, in honor of the Ukrainian nationalist leader who had been assassinated) and thousands of Jews were murdered. It was immediately clear that Ukrainian militias were involved in this operation, together with the Germans.

By 1945, the Jews had disappeared from Lviv. The USSR moved the Polish population to the new Poland and brought in the Ukrainians, who until then had lived in the countryside. Lviv became a different city from what it had been for centuries. Ukrainians came to live in the houses of the Poles and the Jews. They were mainly Greek-Catholic but in 1946 they were forced to join the Orthodox Church in Moscow because being Russian Orthodox provided a greater guarantee of loyalty to the Kremlin. The Greek-Catholic Church survived in hiding and amid harsh persecutions until 1989, when it came back into the open. Lviv was one of the centers of the fight for Ukrainian independence. It was said, regarding the process of the liberation of Ukraine, that Lviv was like Piedmont during the *Risorgimento*.[73]

In this age of nationalism, one ethnic group has not been involved, the Romani people, possibly because it does not have land or an elite. They have always lived with and been hated by

---

73. Cf. Carlo Ossola, "Leopoli, città di sogni e di confini annullati," *Il Sole 24 ore*, May 21, 2017, 6.

European populations. Even today, it continues particularly in the context of their lives on the edge of society. The Porrajmos, which was the murder of the Romani and the Sinti who were deported, sterilized, and killed in the Nazis gas chambers, did not have much impact on this widespread attitude of hatred of the Romani people, the "innocent enemy."[74]

The Nation and the Teaching of Hatred

During this period of nationalism, in particular in the twentieth century, national identities overwhelmingly occupied political and international life. Umberto Eco encouraged us not to forget that to construct a national identity and then spread it among people involved inventing an enemy through the teaching of hatred.[75] So for the French and the Belgians, the Germans were called *boche*. For the Italian soldiers during World War I, Slovenians, and Croatians were called *crucchi* because they asked for *kruch*, that is, bread. We could also talk about the prejudices and the derisive definitions regarding the Italians, especially after their massive emigration to America and various countries in Europe.

Perhaps the most evident case of the construction of the enemy is anti-Semitism, which is based on centuries of prejudice, including strong religious prejudice. It is important to remember that the Jews were the only religious minority in Europe living together with the Christians, who were the majority. The Muslims or people of other religions had been dramatically eliminated. Jews and Judaism, as it

---

74. Cf. Christian Bernadac, *Sterminateli! Adolf Hitler contro i nomadi d'Europa* (La Spezia: Fratelli Melita, 1988).
75. Umberto Eco, *Inventing the Enemy* (Boston: Houghton Mifflin Harcourt, 2012)

is well-known, were the main focus of the Nazis' hatred.[76] Anti-Semitism, however, still exists.[77] Not only do totalitarian and openly anti-Semitic regimes endorse the hatred of Jews, but this attitude, and this is an important and worrying sign, often appears in democratic or Bonapartist regimes. When the Chief Rabbi of Rome, Riccardo Di Segni, was commemorating the eleven victims of the Pittsburg synagogue bombing in 2018, he said there is no country in the world where Jews can consider themselves safe.[78]

Nationalities seem to be immutably deep-rooted, regardless of whether their history is long or not. In 1915, in the middle of World War I and raging nationalism, Pope Benedict XV, an acute observer of the events taking place in Europe, called the war a "useless massacre" and said, "Nor let it be said that the immense conflict cannot be settled without the violence of war. Lay aside your mutual purpose of destruction; remember that Nations do not die; humbled and oppressed, they chafe under the yoke imposed upon them, preparing a renewal of the combat, and passing down from generation to generation a mournful heritage of hatred and revenge."[79]

Benedict XV considered it necessary for the countries, with their different and opposing interests, to negotiate.

---

76. Cf. Hannah Arendt, *Antisemitism: Part one of the Origins of Totalitarianism* (San Diego: Harcourt Brace Jovanovich: 1985, 1968). See also, Philippe Burrin, *Nazi Anti-Semitism: From Prejudice to the Holocaust* (New York: New Press, 2005).
77. Cf. Léon Poliakov, *The History of Anti-Semitism*, four volumes (Philadelphia: University of Pennsylvania Press, 1955–1984).
78. *Cerimonia di commemorazione delle vittime dell'attentato alla sinagoga di Pittsburgh*, in www.radioradicale.it/ scheda/556327/cerimonia-di-commemorazione-delle-vittime-dellattentato-alla-sinagoga-di-pittsburgh.
79. Benedetto XV, *Allorché fummo chiamati. Esortazione apostolica*, in AAS7 (1915), 365–368. https://www.vatican.va/content/benedict-xv/en/apost_exhortations/documents/hf_ben-xv_exh_19150728_fummo-chiamati.html

He was convinced that "nations do not die" but they pass "down from generation to generation a mournful heritage of hatred and revenge."[80] This belief was fully confirmed by what happened during World War II. It is interesting to see how the language of hatred in the propaganda of World War I became part of politics, as did Italian victimism, [defined as victimhood, victim mentality, or mentality of grievance] which referred to the "mutilated victory" (the fact that the Kingdom of Italy's claims were not acknowledged). This language of hatred was communicated through fascism and its political language and became one of the bases of fascism. Victimism is used to increase hatred of other people. In murdering the Jews, the Nazis described themselves as the victims of a Jewish conspiracy, which led to the war. Therefore, by eliminating the Jews, they appeared to be defending Germany. One of the most paradoxical effects of victimism is that it deprived the Jews of their reality as victims of the Nazi's policy, by stating the opposite, that it was the Germans who were the victims of the Jews.

At the end of World War II, after Auschwitz and Hiroshima, it seemed, at least for a while, that the period of national hatred was, if not over, in any case not so clear. The Europe of the Six, as a result of the reconciliation between France and Germany, was starting the process of European integration, which was to place national identities on a single horizon. In the meantime, goods and people began to circulate freely across the borders. Europe's nationalist wars seemed to be buried forever.

In the West, during the Cold War, we forgot the strength and the deep-rootedness of the national identities of East-

---

80. Cf. Roberto Morozzo della Rocca, *Le nazioni non muoiono: Russia rivoluzionaria, Polonia indipendente e Santa Sede* (Bologna: Il Mulino, 1992).

ern Europe. These identities had apparently been crushed by Marxist ideology and by communist politics, as by an enormous sheet of ice. However underneath it, the national identities were seething. With the fall of the Berlin Wall, at the end of the communist regimes, the national identities reemerged with surprising and sometimes devastating vitality, which resulted in various conflicts. The most painful of those was the end of former Yugoslavia.

Sarajevo remains a symbol of national and ethnic hatred. In a long siege that lasted from 1992 to 1996, out of a population of around three hundred thousand, twelve thousand people died. The composition of the population changed completely: in 1921, over 20 percent were Serbs, and afterward, they were half that number; the number of Croatian Catholics fell dramatically; that of Muslims increased. The ten thousand Jews in 1921 were reduced to less than seven hundred after the Holocaust.[81]

It is important to remember that after World War II, and in particular since the 1960s, with decolonization, the world map changed. New states were created based on lines drawn arbitrarily by the colonizers, and often founded without considering historical legacy, traditions, religions, and ethnicities. The nationalism and national hatred that appeared in the second half of the twentieth century seemed to be of greater importance in the Global South, more so than in the Europe of the Cold War.

The most dramatic event in this case was the partition of the British Raj, part of the British Empire, with the creation of India and Pakistan (a totally new nation, designed on the basis of its population being Muslim and not wanting to remain

---

81. Norman M. Naimark, *Fires of Hatred. Ethnic Cleansing in Twentieth-Century Europe* (Cambridge, MA: Harvard University Press, 2002).

an Islamic minority in a sea of Hindus). One of the many new decolonized nations of the second half of the twentieth century was South Africa. Despite the violence of apartheid, Nelson Mandela's South Africa was a different case since it did not carry out any ethnic cleansing and remained a country with many ethnic groups. In 1994, South Africa became a multicultural nation, referred to as the Rainbow Nation, an expression coined by the Anglican Archbishop Desmond Tutu, the first black man in this position.

Overcoming Hatred in the Global World

At the time of the fall of the Berlin Wall, nationalism and national hatred were considered less of a central issue in people's lives. The global world, with the end of walls, the opening of borders and markets, the movement of populations, and closer communication generated a different attitude in people—greater consideration for the other. At the same time, it made people feel vulnerable and wonder about their identity: who are we and who is everyone else?

In an introduction to an essay on *Inventing the Enemy*, Umberto Eco talked about how he was once in a taxi in New York and the taxi driver, who was from Pakistan, asked him where he was from. After finding out that he was Italian, where strangely enough for him, people did not speak English, he asked who our enemies were. Eco explained that we were not at war with anyone, that we had not had a war for fifty years, and that the stories of hatred had faded away. Eco said, "He was not satisfied. How can a country have no enemies?"[82] It is certainly true, Eco added, that after the dissolution of the "Evil Empire," the Soviet Union, the United

---

82. Eco, *Costruire il nemico*, 9. Extract from the book *Inventing the Enemy* by Umberto Eco. Harvill Secker (6 Sept. 2012) (translated

States was in danger of losing its identity. After the greatly desired destruction of Carthage by the Romans, people also said, "What will Rome be without Carthage?"

The "Jo Cox" Commission's report, which was also approved by the XVII Italian legislature,[83] shows that today in Europe, hatred, intolerance, xenophobia, and racism represent a problem. It has reappeared in an attitude of "fear of history," as Mircea Eliade said, even in countries with a strong historical identity.[84] Now however, Macron's France, which is true to the national French culture that considers identity as voluntary and not an ethnic fact, is doubting its ability to assimilate its immigrants, especially the Muslims, and is closing its borders. The Visegrád (Czech Republic, Hungary, Poland, Slovakia) countries' policy regarding this question is very clear-cut.

It seems, unfortunately, that a demand for "differentiation" and therefore for protection of their identity, comes from displaced populations throughout the world, involved in events and dramas that we knew nothing about until a few decades ago. This can be seen in the success of sovereigntist, populist movements, whose basis is the defense of their identity with respect to other people. People wonder whether immigration is turning into an invasion. Incitement to hatred feeds on different reports of incidents suffered by certain groups, whether inside or outside their borders. It has its roots in the fear people are experiencing these days.[85]

---

by Stuart Gilbert). https://medium.com/@richardjones_42477/inventing-the-enemy-5a53ff923c4c..

83. Camera dei Deputati, *Commissione Jo Cox sui fenomeni di odio intolleranza xenofobia e razzismo*, Rome 2017.
84. Cf. Mircea Eliade, *Il mito dell'eterno ritorno* (Rome: Lindau, 2007), 137–157.
85. Cf. Pierre-André Taguieff, *Illusione populista* (Milan: Mondadori, 2003).

Fear comes from loneliness in a world that has become very big and has lost its family, religious, and political networks. Fear comes from ignorance when dealing with worlds that we had no contact with before. We hear about them through preconceived prejudice and not through meeting people and learning about their culture. This fear is a vast space, like the internet, and the urban peripheries that we need to support. We need to take action, we need to regulate it, but it is also a world that we need to understand. So much of this fear comes from the loneliness that drives people to adopt identities different from other people's, from not being able to interpret this modern world, from fear of the present time, and from the lack of means to interpret it all.

The reemergence of nationalism and its hatred is an old- and old-fashioned answer that looks as though it is reassuring but in fact throws people into a vortex of fear and violence. It is an answer that, in some cases, can prepare and motivate war. The reassurance of being able to identify the enemy does not make our life better, it does not protect it, instead it poisons society. Being in contact with others and knowing the surrounding culture helps people interpret the present time. It is not a panacea, but an instrument for calming fear, for protecting an innocent enemy, and for working for a more hospitable world. As part of the global world, it is important to learn to experience all aspects of life in our towns and cities of our nation, in a new, empathetic, and cultured way.

Four
The Resistance of the Righteous in the Darkness of the Holocaust

An Event in History Never to Be Forgotten

The Holocaust is slowly slipping into the past, like every historical event does over time. The witnesses who did so much to help us understand the extent of the tragedy are disappearing, and now it seems to be linked to past worlds, to Nazism and to "Old Europe." People who want to make it relevant today, look for victims who make them think of that tragedy, encouraged by the widespread victimism of our times. This way the Holocaust becomes a metaphor, whereas in fact it is an incredibly harsh, real history. The Holocaust is a combination of an insane ideology, political decisions, widespread complicity, murderous fanaticism, the use of technology, and systematic cruelty, which led to the assembly-line style murder of six million Jews.

Does our memory fade? When we go to Auschwitz, our amnesia disappears immediately. When you walk around the concentration camp that annihilated over one million lives, you can feel its cruel history. There, history continues to speak to us, through a heavy, dark silence. During the interfaith prayer organized "in the spirit of Assisi" by the Community of Sant'Egidio in Krakow in 2009, I had the privilege of being with Giuseppe Laras, who was the Chief Rabbi of Milan for twenty-five years, when he went to the concentration camp where his mother and his grandmother were killed. In the face of this persecution, he whispered: "I never hurt anyone; why should others hurt me?" His mother and his grandmother were arrested on October 2, 1944, by two Italian SS soldiers who had been tipped off by the janitor (who received 5,000 liras for each woman). His mother bravely managed to make him run away in time. Laras said: "I remember the last time I and my mother looked at each other, after that I never saw her again. I remember the desperate rush to find a safe place to hide. I remember that I did not say a word for over six months. My mother was beautiful, she was my mother. My family was beautiful, with the enormity of life that is gently hidden and summed up in the word "family." My childhood was beautiful too but on October 2nd, 1944, when I was nine years old, I lost it all. It was an irreversible loss. When I am asleep, particularly upset and stressed, I still hear them banging hard on the door and I wake up with a start."[86]

In Auschwitz, standing next to Rabbi Laras, who was silent, serious, and composed, nobody spoke. There was only the feeling of the terrible weight on the shoulders of this man and of so many men and women like him. This is the weight of history, forced into the hearts of our continent. I will never forget it.

This did not only happen in Auschwitz, but also in the other concentration camps I have visited. I remember Majdanek, near Lublin, where among others, sixty thousand Jews were killed. The camp was almost completely destroyed. What struck me there was the enormous open urn under a roof, containing the ashes and a few bones found in the crematorium oven when Majdanek was liberated.[87] Humanity reduced to ashes. The deniers (the first of whom were the

---

86. Giuseppe Laras, "Quella fragile bellezza che sconfigge il male," December 5, 2017, in www.luoghidellinfinito.it/Pagine/Quella-fragile-bellezza-che-sconfigge-il-male.aspx.
87. Tomasz Kranz, *Extermination of Jews at the Majdanek Concentration Camp* (Lublin: Państwowe Muzeum na Majdanku, 2007, 2nd ed. revised 2010).

Nazis themselves) wanted to reduce the memory to dust but, as Donatella Di Cesare wrote, and I completely agree with her, "The ashes are the essence of Europe's existence, of its past and its future."[88]

In, Jasenovac, in Croatia, twenty thousand Jews were murdered alongside a great number of Serbs and Romani people. The perpetrators of this bloody, barbaric savagery were the Croatian Ustashas. Jasenovac was the result of anti-Semitism, nationalism and religious hatred of the Jews and the Orthodox Serbians. Much has been destroyed there out of contempt for historical memory.

These fragile places of suffering still speak to us. The witnesses' personal accounts were about their different experiences but all concerned the same evil events that took place during the war. The Holocaust did not take place because of the war: The cause was Nazism, which consolidated the hatred of the Jews deriving from European nationalisms and sometimes from afar. It is no coincidence that the Holocaust took place after the genocide of the Armenians and the Christians in the Ottoman countries during World War I.[89]

War is the perfect situation for carrying out genocides. I am saying this in a period in which unfortunately, warlike, and openly threatening language is being used between countries: they are not at all interested in holding onto the threads of peace and coexistence because these are no longer the ideal to strive for in international relations. Warmon-

---

88. Donatella Di Cesare, *Se Auschwitz è nulla. Contro il negazionismo* (Turin: Einaudi, 2012), 46. Donatella Di Cesare, *If Auschwitz is Nothing: Against Denialism*, trans. David Broder (Cambridge, UK: Polity, 2023).
89. Antonia Arslan, *La masseria delle allodole* (Milan: Rizzoli, 2004). First American ed., Antonia Arslan, *Skylark Farm*, trans. Geoffrey Brock (New York: Knopf, 2006). See also my own book, *La strage dei cristiani*.

gering makes us slide down a slippery slope and we cannot control events, even if we think we do have everything under control. We have forgotten the horrors of war too much.

I will talk about the resistance of the righteous but not without reiterating the unfathomable, inexplicable evil of the Holocaust. I cannot talk about the righteous in order to try and lessen the deep echo of this evil. People sometimes, to console themselves, say, Evil things did happen, but a lot of people did good! There is a vast disproportion between the evil that is done and the reality of the good. It emphasizes the courage of the righteous without reducing the consciousness of the abyss of evil.

We have to be challenged. If it is true that it is impossible to remember all our history, so is it also true that there are important facts of the past that relate to the future. We cannot fill the minds and hearts of tomorrow's generations with the burden of our memories because those young people would probably not be prepared to accept them. Nonetheless, the memory of the Holocaust is an essential point of reference, to be passed down. Even Israel, whose religion is based so much on memory, tells the Jews to pass down one story in particular—one of many: "Be careful that you do not forget the LORD, who brought you out of Egypt, out of the land of slavery" (Deuteronomy 6:12). Every culture or community, if it wants to continue to exist, chooses an essential memory and passes it down to the next generation.

A European History

The Holocaust is the history of our countries. It is not just German and Nazi, as is often said, even though it was Hitler's Germany that massacred German, Polish, Ukrainian, Belorussian, Baltic, and other European Jews. With an insatiable thirst for death, Germany drove the invaded countries to lead their Jews to their death. The Holocaust is not just German history, it is also a European one. The collaborators of the Holocaust, the organizers, the informers, the anti-Semites, came from Italy, France, Poland, Belgium, Holland, Hungary, Croatia, Ukraine, Slovakia, Romania, Bulgaria, and other countries.

Between the two wars, in many countries, Jews were isolated by racist laws well before the Holocaust. In Italy, Mussolini's racist laws led to their isolation,[90] and from September 1943, these laws made it possible to deport over six thousand eight hundred Jews to concentration camps (most of whom never came back) and to kill 322 others.[91] This persecution began earlier in other countries. In 1920, the Hungarian Parliament introduced a restriction on the number of Jewish students for its universities. In Romania, the Jews obtained their civil rights in 1924; however, in 1934, these rights began to be reduced so much so that, in 1938, the Jews were excluded from politics, the economy and culture. In Germany, in 1935, the Nuremberg Laws stated that German Jews were no longer "citizens of the Reich."

According to the most recent estimates, during the Holocaust in Nazi occupied former Soviet Union, around one million six hundred thousand Jews were murdered. However, there was a "Holocaust before Hitler," documented by the historian Jeffrey Veidlinger. The perpetrators at that time were Ukrainians and Poles: It was a series of pogroms against the Jews who were accused of being communists or

---

90. Andrea Riccardi and Gabriele Rigano, eds., *La svolta del 1938, Fascismo, cattolicesimo, antisemitismo* (Milan: Guerini e Associati, 2020).
91. Liliana Picciotto, *Il Libro della memoria: gli ebrei deportati dall'Italia (1943–1945)* (Milan: Mursia, 2017) 7th ed., reports the data on the deportations: 6,806 Jews deported in Nazi camps (of them, 5,969 were killed) and 322 Jews were killed in Italy.

capitalists and of having become rich at the expense of the population. Veidlinger wrote, "The German propaganda, reviving the themes prevailing during the civil war, convinced many people to blame the Jews."[92] This was how the wave of pogroms continued and its perpetrators were soon included in the plan to eliminate the Jews in Eastern Europe.

This part of European history came to a climax with the Wannsee Conference in January 1942, which took place in a luxurious villa on the outskirts of Berlin, and was led by the leader of the SS, Reinhard Heydrich and Adolf Eichmann, who drew up the minutes of the meeting, now available to the public. After the war, Eichmann escaped to Argentina, and in 1960, he was caught by the Mossad and then tried and hanged in Jerusalem. His trial, as we know, led to a wider awareness of the Holocaust. The Wannsee Conference marked the Europeanization of the extermination of the Jews: in fact, it was there that it was decided to hunt down Jews everywhere throughout the whole of Europe.

Before Wannsee, as we have seen, the massacres were carried out in Eastern Europe, but after the conference there was a systematic plan to deport and murder all the Jews in Europe. This is what was written in the text, in its stone-cold, bureaucratic way: "Now, within the framework of the final solution of the Jewish question... in the East the Jews should be used in tasks considered most appropriate. Set up in large columns divided by gender, those fit to work will be made in these areas to build roads. During this operation most of them will succumb to natural causes. The core of those who do survive all this, and they are so gifted in resistance, should be treated in an adequate manner. They are the best product of natural selection and if let free, should be seen as a germ cell of a new Jewish revival (as seen in the past).

---

92. Veidlinger, *In the Midst of Civilized Europe*.

Within the framework... of the final solution, Europe will be combed clean from West to East...."[93]

On February 15, 1942, the first trains packed with Jews arrived in Auschwitz from Silesia, and they were immediately gassed. The destruction machinery was set up and schedules were organized. Christopher Browning, an American scholar, said that in March 1942, between 75 percent and 80 percent of the Jews in Europe were still alive and 20–25 percent had already died; eleven months later, in February 1943, the percentage was the other way round. Just over 20 percent were still alive and condemned to a very precarious life.[94]

The process of unifying Europe started from the deep-seated refusal to accept that these events could be repeated and from the desire to write a completely different story. One of the moral limits to unifying Europe is not having paid sufficient attention to the impact of what took place in Auschwitz on our democracies. Europe emerged from the abyss of Auschwitz and its foundation is the rejection of everything that led to the Holocaust. The mixture of a criminal process, nationalism, anti-Semitism, totalitarianism, and fascism are still present in Europe and in the rest of the world, supported by conspiracy theories and denial, which are popular among people who are disoriented by globalization. All this creates the illusion that hatred is a guarantee of safety or that it can explain our complex world. We must have the courage to identify and remember the terrible ingredients of this story and firmly refute them, one by one, if we want to make our history different and avoid the possible risks of going back to the past.

---

93. Cf. Peter Longerich, *Wannsee: The Road to the Final Solution*, trans. Lesley Sharpe (Oxford: Oxford University Press, 2021).
94. Christopher R. Browning, *Ordinary Men: Reserve Police Battalion 101 and the Final Solution in Poland* (New York: Harper Perennial, 2017). Kindle ed. position 40 on 4694.

Our memory is our only guarantee for a peaceful and democratic Europe. It is no coincidence that David Sassoli[95] came with the President of the European Commission, Ursula Von der Leyen, in 2021, to Fossoli, a holding site active until August 1944, for Italian Jews who were then deported and murdered. In his last non-institutional trip, the President of the European Parliament, thinking about the Holocaust, said:

> What happened is a result of societies aware of human rights but unable to make them prevail against prejudice and hatred. Even peace-loving societies, but unable to uproot the pandemic of war. Societies that believed themselves better than their neighbor, exasperating antagonism that turned the love for their own country into fanatical and criminal nationalism.

Then, referring to today with a worried expression, he added:

> What is taking place now in Europe is worrying: discrimination, violence, attacks on the legal system, on the freedom of press. All of this is intolerable for us and cannot be reconciled with our values. We have unprecedented sanctions, and we want to use them.[96]

The Collaborators of Evil

The first massacre in Italy began on the banks of Lake Maggiore on September 13–14, 1943. Most of the victims were non-Italian Jews. Most Italian Jews did not feel alarmed yet, but the collaborators of evil were already emerging. Some

---

95. The former President of the European Parliament.
96. David Sassoli, "Preoccupano attacchi alla democrazia, restiamo vigili," in www.ansa.it/sito/notizie/mondo, July 11, 2021.

Italians guided the Germans in their hunt for the Jews. Others received money to disclose their whereabouts or hunted them down themselves. These were people with no humanity, full of anti-Semitic contempt, fanatical, greedy people according to whom even a Jewish child could not be considered a child but was either someone without the right to live or else merely a way to make money. This child was an Untermensch, subhuman. The Nazis found people all over Europe who were prepared to believe it.[97]

The Holocaust is part of the history of Rome, the city I come from. Its streets witnessed the "Black Saturday" of October 16, 1943, when the Jews were fleeing from the German raid, carried out by the Nazis who were holding the addresses of the Jewish homes in their hands. My grandmother remembered that day she was walking near the old ghetto and saw a little Jewish boy who seemed to be waving at her from an open truck. After the raid on October 16, many Jews were reported or handed over for money: 5,000 liras for a man, 3,000 liras for a woman, and 1,000 liras for a child. More money was given in exchange for the community leaders. The SS officer, Herbert Kappler, said, for what it is worth, that after the first raid on Rome, the Germans almost always acted on tip-offs from the Italians.

In the hunt for the Jews, an evil, greedy, vengeful, fanatical Italy emerges. Nonetheless, it was basically absolved after the war, thanks to the myth of "Italians, the good people." Fanaticism was very common. Two days after the armistice, Giovanni Pestolozza, a collaborator of Giovanni Preziosi, who signed the Manifesto of Race, reported to the Germans that three wagons full of Jews were escaping to Genoa. Traitors and spies, deceitful go-betweens, collected money for

---

97. Mimmo Franzinelli, "I volenterosi delatori di Hitler," *Il sole 24 ore*, January 23, 2005, 35.

the journey to Switzerland from the Jews and then handed them over to the Germans. Such betrayal lasted to the end of the war throughout Europe. The Nazis ran their death camps at full speed for as long as they could. Even when they were close to being defeated, they continued to murder people with their delusional fanaticism.

In the meantime, the Jews' belongings were being stolen—from things of little value to works of art, houses, jewelry, furniture, all kinds of property. All over Europe there was a green light for people to steal anything and everything that had belonged to the Jews. In Milan, a batch of typewriters endangered the lives of the Levi brothers. In Rome, the shops belonging to the Jews were targeted. When a Roman Jew, called Olga Di Veroli, who was hiding in a convent, went home to get something, the woman who had occupied her apartment started shouting, "fascist, Germans! She's a Jew, get her!" I will not dwell on the question of the stolen property, as it was real plundering and justice has never been fully served.[98]

The Holocaust is a European issue. It is not only German but also a part of Italian history.... I can state that very firmly. Just as it is the history of so many Europeans who acted on their own initiative, out of self-interest or fanaticism. This is how Rabbi Giuseppe Laras described his relatives' attitude with respect to the onslaught of evil: "One was not aware of the fact that the world was upside down and evil." There are times when the world is turned upside down by evil. However, for many Jews, this was unthinkable, so they did not hide. Many non-Jews watched, stunned by the intimidation of the Nazis. The power of evil, with the brutality of the Nazis, intimidated people, made them fear for their lives, and

---

98. Amedeo Osti Guerrazzi, *Gli specialisti dell'odio: Delazioni, arresti, deportazioni di ebrei italiani* (Florence: Giuntina, 2020).

made them feel helpless. Helplessness breeds indifference: this is the phrase that Liliana Segre wanted engraved on the memorial of Platform 21 at the Milan railway station, from where the trains left for the concentration camps.[99]

The Resistance of the Righteous

Was it humanly possible to do something, when there were posters announcing the death penalty for anyone who helped the Jews? When people lived in fear of the Nazis and of the bombings? When they were hungry and there was no food for their families? When they were overwhelmed by just trying to survive? Was it not enough to stay away from fanatics or people who sold human life? More than that seemed impossible.

Yet it was not impossible. Even then, everyone could decide what to do, even when there was little room, and the decision was costly. Both stories of righteous and of evil people began with a decision, in a tumultuous world that was dehumanized by war and by fear. In Rome, on October 16, as I mentioned, the most extensive raid in Italy was carried out: Jewish men, women, children, and the elderly were taken from their homes. At 5.15 a.m., the SS stormed the houses in the ghetto and hunted down the remaining Jews: Nothing was left to chance; everything was planned with implacable ferocity. They rounded up 1,024 people, two hundred of whom were children. Two days later, they left in eighteen sealed wagons. After a terrifying six-day journey the train arrived at Auschwitz. A total of fifteen men and one

---

99. Comunità di Sant'Egidio, ed., *Milano 30 gennaio 194: Memorie della deportazione dal Binario 21* (Milan: Guerini e Associati, 2016).

woman managed to get back to Rome (Settimia Spizzichino, a Roman woman who spoke about her story her whole life).[100]

Seeing the people being rounded up, "a poor woman standing nearby took out her rosary and started to pray and cry, whispering with trembling lips: poor innocent flesh." It was too much; people's emotions overcame their fear. That was how those poor people felt, like the bookseller from the Roman district of Trastevere, in what was then called Viale del Re. He told his daughter, Trieste Melappioni, to run and warn a family of Jews and tell them to escape. A teacher, Amendola, hid her Jewish student in her house because he was running away. He was called Michele Tagliacozzo, and I met him. The Roman priest, Don Libero Raganella, went to cloistered nuns with a forged order to hide Jews. After society had accepted the discrimination of the Jews in 1938, there were many courageous stories within a frightened silence, but most people felt totally helpless.[101]

Some people even fought without weapons against an overwhelming power. Jean Ancel, a researcher at Yad Vashem, talked about the Chief Rabbi of Romania, the young Alexandre Safran, who saved so many Romanian Jews: "His life is an extraordinary example of a fight without weapons ... with as its only source the power of the spirit as opposed to brutal force."[102] Safran was so determined to save his people that he deftly maneuvered among the contradictions of Marshal Ion Antonescu's regime. He collaborated with the apostolic nuncio, Andrea Cassulo, conversed with the queen, with the Orthodox patriarch (who was hostile for a long time, but who was moved when he saw him imploring

---

100. Spizzichino, *Gli anni rubati*.
101. See my own book: *L'inverno più lungo. 1943–44: Pio XII, gli ebrei e i nazisti a Roma* (Rome-Bari: Laterza, 2008).
102. Alexandre Safran, *Lottando nella bufera. Memorie 1939–1947* (Florence: Giuntina, 1995), 23.

on his knees), and others. He was watched by the Germans and only had a narrow margin of action, but he found ways to widen that space with his words. Few Jewish authorities were able to do as much.

Were the non-Jews able to witness so much evil without doing anything? Not everyone was helpless. Many men and women discovered the power of the powerless, as Václav Havel said in the battle against the Czechoslovakian communist regime.[103] The powerless did have power, but exercising it exposed them to risks and could come with a heavy cost. It may have been the offer of a hiding place, a facilitated escape, some information that saved a life.... Some people were moved to act by their participation in the pain of the Jews, others by personal connections, for religious reasons, by a sense of justice, by the conviction that it was just too much.... They were not indifferent; they did not just save themselves. A door that opens for a person or a family is a revolution against evil. The hunt for the Jews was really too much: It was impossible to remain indifferent.

The righteous are not heroes, they are ordinary people who discover the power of the powerless. Regina Bettin, who lived in Padua with her husband and her children, was a nanny for a Jewish family named Sacerdoti, in Venice. She found out that the train the Roman Jews took on October 16 had gone through the Padua station. She immediately contacted Mrs. Sacerdoti, who had been warned not to go back to Venice, and she offered to look after her children, together with her own. She hid them for eight months, despite all the difficulties and the bombing. Today the former nanny is "righteous among the nations."

---

103. Vaclav Havel, et al. *The Power of the Powerless: Citizens Against the State in Central-Eastern Europe*, ed. John Keane (Armonk, NY: M.E. Sharp, Inc., 1985).

Acknowledging the righteous was a great idea of the Yad Vashem memorial in Jerusalem. The definition, "righteous among the nations," has Talmudic origins. According to a Talmudic legend, in every generation there are thirty-six unknown righteous people, on whom the destiny of mankind depends. The figure of the righteous person is an acknowledgment of non-Jews who made a commitment to the Jews during the Holocaust. The country with the most righteous people (over seven thousand two hundred) was Poland, followed by Holland and France. There were over 770 righteous people in Italy and there were also righteous people in countries not involved in the war, like a Portuguese consul who saved thousands of people by granting them visas against government orders, a Turk, two Chinese people, one from Salvador, Muslims, and many others....

Moshe Bejski created the garden of the righteous in Jerusalem. He was a Polish Jew, born in a Jewish town near Krakow. He went through very hard times and experienced the solidarity of some non-Jews and the indifference of others in Krakow. He was deported to Auschwitz and managed to get into the factory that belonged to the German businessman Oscar Schindler, who was a Nazi but became righteous among the nations. Schindler managed to save around 1,200 Jews by having them work in his factory until the camp was freed by the Red Army in May 1945.[104] The film director Stephen Spielberg made this story into a famous film. When Bejski arrived in Israel, he testified to his personal experience and said that a righteous person is neither a saint nor a superman but is an ordinary person with his limitations. He said, "I believe that if many individuals had been able to

---

104. Emilie Schindler, *Io, Emilie Schindler. Una voce dal silenzio* (Barbes: Milan 2008).

make just a small step in favor of the Jews … the number of the saved would have been infinitely higher."[105]

These were ordinary people who made a difference. In fact, the Hebrew text of the *Ethics of the Fathers* says, "When men are lacking, make an effort to be a man yourself."[106] When Ida Brunelli from Monselice (Padua) was eighteen years old, a Hungarian Jewish woman who was dying gave Ida her three children to look after. Ida, in turn, would pretend that they were Catholic refugees in her town. There were also adventurous individuals, like the sales representative Giorgio Perlasca, in Budapest, a staunch fascist, originally from Padua, who pretended to be a delegate of the Spanish Embassy. When four hundred thousand Hungarian Jews disappeared into the death machine, he hid Jews in "safe houses" at the neutral embassies, and in the nunciatures, and used the Spanish law from before 1492 that recognized Jews as citizens of Spain. Enrico Deaglio wrote a book about him, with a very evocative title, *La banalità del bene*. (The banality of good.) [107]

Cloistered monasteries opened up to Jews they had never met before. Much of what happened could not be documented and the records of one monastery say, "The reign of terror established by the Teutonic enemy and based on spying and by fascist meretriciousness … was such as to prevent writing down that which could incriminate."[108]

---

105. Gabriele Nissim, *Il tribunale del bene: La storia di Moshe Bejski, l'uomo che creò il Giardino dei giusti* (Milan: Mondadori, 2003), 159.
106. S. Parenzo, ed., *Massime dei Padri*. [*Pirké Avòt*] (Florence: Giuntina, 2007).
107. Enrico Deaglio, *La banalità del bene. Storia di Giorgio Perlasca* (Milan: Feltrinelli, 2003).
108. Quoted in my: *L'inverno più lungo 1943–44: Pio XII, gli ebrei e i nazisti a Roma* (Bari: Laterza, 2012), 272.

The righteous left few traces except in the memory of the people they saved. Eighty-five percent of the Roman Jews who escaped owed their survival to citizens and religious institutions. By studying their stories, it is also possible to sense the role that was difficult to document, played by the families who hid the Jews, sometimes independently, sometimes in cooperation with their parish. The problems often concerned the question of food and the informers.

The Jews who were hunted down had often lived a comfortable life before. Don Raimondo Viale, from Cuneo, who helped non-Italian Jews who were trapped in Italy, wrote, "There were men and women, women with grey hair, children ... almost all of whom in normal times were used to a comfortable life ... reduced to fleeing like prey followed by dogs and hunters up into mountains." They were forced to depend for everything on the people they met.

Who was that SS captain who spoke to the then young prisoner, Rabbi Elio Toaff, who refused to dig his own grave and who recited the prayer of the dead? He saved him from being shot and one night he opened the prison door: "Raus!" (Get out!) Why did he do that? Some soldiers rebelled. Franz Jägerstätter, a hero, an ardent Catholic Austrian peasant, refused to be a soldier. Opposed by everyone, even the Church, he was only supported by his wife Franziska. He emphatically stated the alternative— "A soldier of Christ or a soldier of Hitler." He was guillotined in August 1943.[109] Hannah Arendt talked about a German Wehrmacht sergeant in Poland, called Anton Schmidt, who had met Jewish partisans and helped them for five months: He was discovered and killed. Moreover, five thousand Jews were saved in Germany, most

---

109. Cesare G. Zucconi, *Cristo o Hitler? Vita del beato Franz Jägerstätter* (Cinisello Balsamo: San Paolo, 2008).

of them in Berlin, the heart of the Nazi's power: How many righteous Germans helped them?

Aharon Applefeld, a Romanian Jew who escaped from a concentration camp and was saved by two criminals who did not know who he was, wrote, "Every man saved during the war is saved thanks to a person who, in a moment of great danger, approached him." He concluded saying, "In the concentration camps we did not meet God, but we met the righteous." The Hungarian Jewish writer Edith Bruck, who describes Italian as the language of freedom, talks about "*piccole luci*" ("tiny lights") that made it possible to survive in the abyss.[110]

No, we must not lose the memory of the Holocaust! It is a way of holding onto the last breath of those who were dying, like what happened to Edith Bruck, who together with other prisoners in the Bergen Belsen concentration camp, was forced to move the corpses. Some people were still alive, and they whispered their name, so they would not be forgotten but remembered by their relatives. They gave her a task: "Tell people, they won't believe it; if you survive, tell them for us too." Holding onto those last breaths and those requests meant remembering the dreadful events that took place and at the same time, the capacity to resist, the power of goodness. Some people, quite a few, resisted because they were convinced that evil is not omnipotent. How important it is, then, to cherish the memory of what is good!

Zygmunt Bauman said: "It does not matter how many people preferred moral duty to the common sense of self-preservation; what is important is some did. Evil is not

---

110. Edith Bruck, *Il pane perduto*, 10th ed. (Milan: La nave di Teseo, 2021).

almighty. It is possible to resist it."[111] This is a lesson for our times and for the future. These are not distant events; remembering them preserves our humanity.

Anyone who saves a life makes history. The phrase in the Hebrew Mishnah, codified by Maimonide, is, "Whoever saves one man saves the whole world." There is a similar expression in the Koran, in the Surah of the Mensa: "Whoever kills a person ... it is as though they killed all of humanity. And whoever vivifies a person, it is as though they gave life to all of humanity." The righteous save the honor of their people; they save humanity.

There remains the terrible awareness of the evil that man can do, of how much evil a system like that of the Nazis can cause. The Nazi's actions were unique and extreme in their desire to systematically destroy an entire population. We want to believe, and we certainly hope, that this amount of evil will never again come to pass. Remembering forces us to grasp processes from the beginning, to consider them as more than myths, so they can be prevented. Sometimes we may be accused of using exaggerated language to describe them, but it is often necessary to exaggerate in order to understand the unimaginable extent of evil. If we do not exaggerate, we do not understand and consequently we do not act. We can and we must fight evil, especially without weapons.

---

111. Zygmunt Bauman, *Modernità e olocausto* (Bologna: Il Mulino, 1992), 280. Zygmunt Bauman, *Modernity and the Holocaust* (Ithaca, NY: Cornell University Press, 1989).

Five

Christians and the Future of Europe

Fear of the Future

In 1942, in the middle of World War II, the greatest Italian philosopher of the twentieth century, Benedetto Croce, who was a liberal layman, wrote an essay with a significant title: "Why we cannot but call ourselves Christians."[112] For him, saying that we were Europeans meant saying that we were Christians, without identifying ourselves as belonging to a church or a religion. We cannot only allude to Europe's Christian and historical roots. We cannot only settle for our Christian roots or our Christian past. We should not only boast about our history, like impoverished aristocratic families.

Christianity is not only the legacy of the past in Europe. Today, the Christian communities, whether numerous or less so, are deeply intertwined with European life, like a unifying network from the Atlantic to the Ural Mountains. There are possibly less Christians in Europe today than in the past, but they live the Gospel, they pray, they listen to the Word of God, they are friends of the poor, they try not to let themselves be closed off within the borders of a small selfish world. They are a resource of humanity, of thoughts, actions and visions that are rooted in the Word of God.

Christians have been active protagonists within Europe's historic and recent unifying processes: the Protestant world

---

112. Benedetto Croce, "Perché non possiamo non dirci cristiani," *La Critica*, vol. 40 (1942), 289–297. View of Articoli varii. Perchè non possiamo non dirci "cristiani" (uniroma1.it)

in the ecumenism after World War I; the Catholic and Protestant world in the process of the unification of Europe after World War II; and the Christian world in resistance to the oppression of Eastern Europe until 1989. European Christians experienced the two European wars of the twentieth century, which soon became world wars, as their defeat. They rose from the depths of despair, from Auschwitz, and dreamt of peace among Europeans. After the Holocaust, Christians cultivated a new relationship with Jews, who have always lived alongside Christians in Europe.

Christianity is not just ancient history; it is the current reality of people who believe in the Lord and live the Gospel. Yet today the Christian communities risk falling ill with a disease that is typical of Europe—fear.

Our societies are full of fear, which is a feeling that some politicians know very well how to use. Europe is afraid of global horizons, which have expanded enormously in recent decades with globalization. Globalization has been a great revolution, and we are only superficially aware of it. Bauman talks about liquid fear, as the demon lurking in the folds of society.[113] Like Micea Eliade said, people are terrified of history. It is as though whatever is far away can reach us at any time and come onto our horizon. The people that this "far away" represents, are often immigrants. So, the perception of these phenomena is emotional: A few years ago, over 70 percent of Italians thought that there were four times more immigrants than their actual number. The same refers to Muslims. Fear leads to demands for reassurance, protection, defense, and in fact borders and walls are then discovered again. Europeans, exposed to the winds of the global world,

---

113. Zygmunt Bauman, *Liquid Fear* (Cambridge, UK: Polity Press, 2006).

are trying to reinvent their identity and defend themselves from what they consider to be excessive contamination.

Europeans are afraid of history, and they do not understand much about who they are in the big wide world. They isolate themselves. Bauman said that fear has made people lose their sense of adventure. Yes, because Europe was, for better or worse, an extrovert continent—from trade to the domination of the world, to the unsustainable idea of having to "civilize" the world, to the desire to discover every part of it, to the missions—and now it is afraid. The consequences are there for everyone to see—people's obsession with material and psychological well-being. We are afraid of having lost control of ourselves and of our environment. Bauman shows how contemporary man feels lonely and defenseless: "The over-evaluation of the individual results in the full emergence of his vulnerability, stripped of the protection once offered by the dense network of social ties."[114]

Community and Family Ties in Europe Are Being Loosened in Favor of Individualism

People are feeling dispossessed and exposed to the world. It is as though the European Union does not protect them in a tangible way. European institutions seem to be very cold and distant. After the Russian attack on Ukraine, European countries feel more exposed to any threats that might come from Russia, also considering their difficult history with the Soviet Union and the Russian Empire.

Thinking of ourselves as Europeans is not easy; it is easier to think in terms of nationalities or territories. Men and women who feel bewildered in a global world take refuge

---

114. Zygmunt Bauman, *Europe: an Unfinished Adventure* (Cambridge, UK: Polity Press, 2004).

in their *heimat* ("homeland") and seem to want to make it impenetrable so it will not be affected by global currents. Fear, anger, and pessimism go together in a time in which politics consists of a lot of emotions. Something profound is happening in Europe, not just in politics, but in people's consciousness. There is a growing distrust of unifying ties, such as the European Union. Harsh and aggressive language is finding popular consensus, even among political leaders in several European countries, and this kind of language has not been heard for a long time. People think that policies with muscles protect them better and that it is right to talk about nationalism, populism, and sovereignism. They also think it is right to look for a strong man as a leader, rather than someone able to mediate and promote democracy. People want to isolate their national destiny from that of the other Europeans.

Fear risks infecting the Christian communities. They can look at the past and see the decrease in the number of believers because of secularization. This is a reason for pessimism. But the problem today is not so much secularization as it is globalization, which makes Europeans, and too many Christians among them, frightened, angry, and pessimistic. This was the prayer of the Italian Christian and poet, David Turoldo: "Oh Lord, save me from the blandness of the grown man and liberate your people from this senility of the spirit. Give us back the ability to cry and to enjoy; bring the people back to sing in Your Churches."[115]

Save us from the blandness and senility of the spirit! We cannot accept the blandness and senility of the Church. Many Christians who are afraid and want to isolate themselves request the Church make the Christian identity sa-

---

115. David Maria Turoldo, *Il sapore del pane* (Cinisello Balsamo: Edizione Paoline, 2012), 11.

cred. This identity distinguishes us from the others, from foreigners, immigrants, Muslims—a request for benediction or the consecration of the borders with respect to Christianity. This sounds like a question about the theology of the nation. Pope John Paul II developed a theology of the nation but in a European context and in the logic of pulling down the Wall in Europe and the walls between Europe and the Southern part of the world. Today we are asking Christianity to sanctify national identities, maybe even walls.

The Gospel Frees Us from Fear, Senility and Conformism

How can we free ourselves from this blandness, senility, and contamination of fear? What can we do? How much do the Christian communities count? There is a sense of irrelevance. It is not just a question of political action, but of starting from oneself, from a change that nobody can prevent. Martin Buber called it the Archimedes point from which one can lift up the world, that is, the transformation of oneself. This is an invitation to convert to the Gospel, the Gospel that says with the words of Christ who had risen, to the women at his tomb, "Do not be afraid, for I know that you are looking for Jesus, who was crucified" (Matthew 28:5). Fear is an insidious feeling that is constantly confirmed by reality. There is always a reason in life and in history to be afraid. It is easy to find! In the Bible however, which recognizes how full of fear we are, there is often the invitation not to be afraid. The Gospel of Jesus frees us of fear with the gift of faith. It opens our heart to reality, to the future, to the coming Kingdom of God.

The first gesture to be made, in a frightened and bewildered Europe, is simple and decisive: to put the Gospel back in the center of our personal and community life, like a light for the path we walk on. It is not easy for adult Christians to convert to the Gospel. As Nicodemus said, and he knew theology very well, "How can a man be born when he is old?" (John 3:4). How can old Christian communities be born again, simply by converting to the Gospel?

As Francis of Assisi said, we must convert to the Gospel, *sine glossa*, without additions, in order to be the light in the house, which is Europe. The first responsibility of Christians in Europe is to convert to the Gospel, and be convinced that in their fragility and weakness, the Gospel is their real strength. The Gospel frees us of personal fear; it transforms our blandness; it drives away Christian-nationalist ideologies; it encourages Christians who are frightened to play a role in European societies. It provides light in the darkness of the future.

How wonderful it would be if everyone went back to the Gospel together, Evangelical Christians, Orthodox Christians, Catholics. It would be wonderful to have a year dedicated by all the European Churches to the Gospel, hearing it again in Europe, asking the Europeans to be enlightened by it, spreading it among our fellow citizens. This is something I have always thought—a year of the Gospel for Christians of all the Churches! The Gospel unites European Christians, despite their different denominations, and drives them toward the search for the future, so they leave the enclosures they have created, often out of fear.

It is not a matter of despising our fellow citizens' fears as though we were superior. We have to make the renewed faith grow, so it can make European Christians raise their heads and free them of the pressure of fear and resignation. Fear seems to be the spirit of our times. Carl Gustav Jung warned that the spirit of the times "is a religion ... of an international character, but with an unappreciated feature of wanting to affirm such criterion of truth.... Thinking differently ...

gives the impression of being wrong...."[116] The Gospel frees us of fear and urges us to be a community— a community, not a tribe around reassuring, muscular leaders.

The first great responsibility of Christians is for the Gospel to once again become fascinating and exciting, and to free us from the dictatorship of the emotions and behavior inspired by self-defense. Together, European Christians have to rediscover that their true wealth is the Gospel of Jesus. This is a rediscovery that has to generate contagious, widespread enthusiasm, between one Church and another, for the Gospel.

The Gospel is not an ideology or politics. It is not a cosmopolitan spirit that wants to betray European countries and make them lose their identity. Today, frightened Europeans say to some Christian leaders, like Pope Francis, and to some Churches, that they have betrayed Christianity in favor of a policy of doing good all over the world, in particular in the third world. The Church is said to have betrayed Christian Europe.... Churches throughout history have been very closely connected to regional and national contexts, and to cities; however, they have always indicated a beyond, a horizon, a wider communion, and then the Kingdom of Heaven.

Nation, Nationalism, and the Weakened Power of Christianity

Churches have taught us to love our land, but not in idolatry. Naturally, I know they sometimes also burned incense to the idols of nationalism, totalitarianism, even racism. However, today they have come a long way and they have freed themselves from that temptation, also because of the

---

116. Carl G. Jung, *Realtà dell'anima* (Turin: Bollati Boringhieri, 1970), 13.

testimony and blood of the martyrs, who in faith resisted nationalisms and totalitarianisms. The martyrs were the strong and silent masters, in the terrible twentieth century in Europe, with its wars and nationalisms.

Today, especially after decades of ecumenism, the Churches, in their diversity, are connected at a European level; they have mixed their histories; they have met and do not let themselves be divided by walls. Nonetheless, as we can also see in several European countries, nationalism is a virus that can divide Churches. In the face of war, Christians sometimes become divided, and so do the Churches. As early as 1872, the Council of Constantinople condemned "excessive" nationalism, which they called phyletism, that promoted the organization of Churches on an ethnic and national basis.

Communion between Churches is a strong bond and should be rediscovered as a constitutive reality of Europe. The reality of sister Churches encourages the brotherhood of peoples. People are not very interested in operations at the top, of meetings between the clergy. The more the Christian communities are sisters (that is, return to the Gospel together, love the poor, cultivate love among one another), the more populations will be brothers.

Conversion to the Gospel and to faith are at the heart of a revival of the prophecy of the Churches and of Christians in Europe. As Pope Francis is preaching, it is a faith that, even through so many difficulties, is coming out of the closed circuits of our temples and our ecclesiastic circles, and is spreading an opportunity for communication and encounter, not a feeling of weariness or blandness. This is the simple secret of life in a Europe that is lost in complexity. Our strength is not powerful or influential communities, not control of the media, not our impact on politics, but in the saving and captivating power of the Gospel of Jesus. If we do not embrace this strength, which is so special, we become insignificant, running away from history, maybe to withdraw in a spiritual bubble or an ecclesiastical retreat.

Small communities, not powerful, but real, in the diaspora, in the corners of our European cities, and on the outskirts. The Lord answered Paul: "My power is made perfect in weakness" (2 Corinthians 12:9). The apostle experiences this message fully, so much so that he said: "For when I am weak, then I am strong" (2 Corinthians 12:10). The weakness of the communities, which in any case is relative, is the ground where the power of the Lord and of the Gospel manifest themselves. I say "relative" because while, over the last few years, societies have lost many forms of participation and many social networks have become much looser, despite all their limitations, Christians are still a community.

Not frightened Christians but strong ones! What does strong mean? Not aggressive, but men and women who, in the corners of Europe, are able to become a shelter for so many people who are seeking, suffering, asking. Strong in God's love, able to communicate it in a personal meeting, in free friendship with people. I think we have to ask ourselves and our brothers to engage ourselves in a daily conversation with our fellow citizens, to listen to their fears, but also convey hope. Above all to be friends, because fear is the daughter of lonely people, who think too much about themselves. The Church has a charisma of friendship: Christianity, through us, should find itself again a friend of the men and women of our time. Christians are called to be the "men and women of the people," talking to everyone, friends with everyone. That is the way I like to interpret the Italian word "*laico*," which as is known, comes from Greek and means "of the people." However, there is a drive to become clerical within an ecclesiastical bubble, almost as if to flee from the contradictions of society and of the effort of widespread friendship.

The Prophecy of Gratuitousness

In a world of diaspora, with people of different religions, different feelings, in the unstable flow of relationships, the humanity of Christian men and women, their faces and their words are the place where there is friendship, where we can hear the echo of the Word of God among the words of men and in their life. Prophetic communities mean above all communities that can speak, converse, and meet everyone. They can pull down the walls of prejudice and fear, of contempt and aggression, while fostering encounters. These communities are signs; signs that indicate both a human way and the Gospel of Jesus. Why is it like that? For no other reason than the grace of the Gospel—that is, gratuitously. The Christian responsibility is to remember, while we are alive, that in Europe it is not all just a question of economy, profit, and money. There is much more than that!

The Christian communities are a space for gratuitousness in a society dominated by money, where everything is bought and sold, where everything has a price. The gratuitousness of the Church, that of the life of Christians and their relationships, are a prophecy and a protest of the society of money. In fact, the Gospel, experienced, proclaimed, and communicated, preserves people's humanity: Free from the obsession of love of oneself, it unites us with other brothers and sisters within a mission; it commits us to live not only for ourselves but for He who died and rose again for us, for the others, for the poor. Free of fear, of the obsessive concern with money, Christians linked together can be witnesses of happiness. Witnesses of happiness in an unhappy society: "It is more blessed to give than to receive" (Acts 20:35) is the secret of the Gospel, which counters the spirit of our times so much and so gently.

The love for the weakness and gratuitousness of Christian life is expressed particularly in the link between the poor and Christians, between the poor and humble people. To use the words of the prophet Zephaniah the wrong way but effectively: "But I will leave within you the meek and humble" (Zephaniah 3:12). It is not just a question of offering assistance, not even if refined. We have often risked a too institutional and professional vision of our relationship with the poor: The Church's works are fine, but ... It is a question of really putting the poor at the center of our community and personal life, in a generous and sympathetic manner. We must learn to be personally close to the poor. They are not only assisted by the community, but they become friends. When we spend time with the poor, we discover their great dignity and their story, and many prejudices and fears disappear.

According to chapter 25 of the teachings of Matthew, in poor people, in foreigners, who are hungry, thirsty, prisoners, homeless ... the disciples see the presence of their master. An Orthodox theologian, Olivier Clément, spoke of the "sacrament of the poor." A specific responsibility of Christians in Europe is to be close to the poor, to love and support them and their friends. The poor are the first friends of the Church. The presence of the poor, even if not always through religious words, speaks of the Gospel and of another way of life. The poor have their own prophecy.

Europe has aged and among the poor there are many old people who are often condemned to loneliness after a life spent among others. By now, too many old people see the ultimate destiny of their existence as being alone or ending up lonely in a retirement home, conceivably after having had a long life with their family in their own home. I think about the homeless, people who are sick with all sorts of diseases, prisoners, the disabled. A society based on money constantly creates too many excluded people. I also think of the Romani people, despised and who became victims of the racism of the forgotten Romani Holocaust, the *Porrajamos*, during which five hundred thousand Romani people died. The Romani people are the only European population that has never claimed land or experienced nationalism. Europe has been their space, where they have often lived as guests.

An Ecumenical Civilization: Living with the Others, for the Other and for the Poorest

In our friendship with the poor, a culture of solidarity personally experienced, put into action and thought out, flows from the heart of the communities. This culture unsettles the European consciousness because it reminds us that men and women are made of weaknesses, that their humanity, above all else, is of value. The connection with the poor gives meaning to life and shows that not everything is money and self-affirmation. Christians live, but they think too: they read; they talk to each other; they have discussions. The engagement in caring for the poor sets people's lives in motion and at the same time it reduces our utilitarian visions, our economistic mechanisms. It disturbs the life of individuals but also society's established and widespread mentality. Christians are a reserve of humanity and solidarity with the poor in Europe.

A Church that is a friend of the poor sees the reality of so many refugees and immigrants. Europeans' fear has found in foreigners the figure that represents the global and invasive world: They embody the fear of history that is developing in our little world. We only see immigrants when they come onto the European horizon, at our borders or in the Mediterranean. What is their life like?

Walls are being built in Eastern Europe to stop immigrants and refugees. And yet, the global world was born with the fall of the Berlin Wall. At that time, there was this idea that there would be a world in which people traveled freely, goods circulated easily, and in which democracy would spread. Globalization represented freedom, but now it is frightening. Today we feel that we must defend ourselves from the refugees and from the poor, rather than protect them.

What is the refugees' story? For many young Africans, emigrating is the greatest adventure (perhaps gamble) of their life, that takes them along routes through the desert and across the sea. We know what happens in the camps in Libya. How many wars, environmental dramas, how much hunger and misery do the migrants go through? Many refugees have no means to survive in their countries where there is no future for them. For example, the many Afghans who adhered to the model of a Western life, and invested in it, now feel like foreigners in their own country, under the Taliban regime, or they are forced to flee. The West intervened heavily in Afghanistan, and then completely forgot about them after withdrawing from the country.

Christians do not only welcome people because they are merciful, which is important to know; they are also reasonable Europeans who know that our countries, with the decrease in population, need the manpower the immigrants can provide. What would become of an old country like Hungary with its wall, without immigrants in thirty years? What would Italy, that is so afraid of the arrival of foreigners, be like with its demographic crisis? Christians also must be active in the integration process of immigrants because it is not enough to let them into the country. In fact, it is the communities that integrate rather than the institutions. European Christians are experts in humanity. The Church, throughout history, has integrated several populations in Europe. The Church has, in its chromosomes, what the Patriarch Bartholomew of Constantinople calls an "ecumenical civilization." *Ecumene* is "the home where we all live," not a place where a few dominate and fight.

Being friends with immigrants is a responsibility of acceptance, but it is also an act of responsibility toward Europe. At least in part, Europe needs new workers because of its demographic crisis. We cannot close the doors in the name of the preservation of Christian identity. Let us not forget the many Christian immigrants who come to our countries and invigorate our communities! Fear comes from far away. In 1989, Pope John Paul said with sorrow, "Many borders tend to close." He then said, "To welcome the other is not for the believer merely... natural attention to his fellow man... for in every human being he knows that he encounters Christ." He concluded forcefully, giving an original interpretation of what it means to be a Catholic: "Catholicity is not only expressed in the fraternal communion of the baptized, but also in the hospitality extended to the stranger, whatever his religious belief."[117]

A fundamental problem for Europe is its relationship with Africa. We have to help young Africans find a future in their countries. Cooperation is necessary in order to do this, but also politicians that are able to convince the African leaders to commit to a policy of development that meets young

---

117. John Paul II, Message for the 85th World Migration Day 1999, https://www.vatican.va/content/john-paul-ii/en/messages/migration/documents/hf_jp-ii_mes_22021999_world-migration-day-1999.html).

people's vital needs. The question of immigration, with the increase in the population in Africa, is very complex and cannot be solved in a simple way, for example, with a wall! Europe and Africa have to think about their future together from this point of view. It is a European issue and not only one that concerns the Mediterranean countries. Christianity, which has its roots in Europe but is vital in Africa, is itself a bridge between the two continents.

Philippe Jenkins, an American historian of religions, when writing about twenty-first century Christianity, talked about a "Third Church," to underline how global Christianity is increasingly taking on an African face: "In contrast with the myth, a typical Christian is not a big white cat belonging to the United States or Western Europe, rather someone poor, often incredibly poor according to Western standards ... whereas Africa assumes its position as the main center of the religion." Jenkins said, "Christianity is flourishing wonderfully among the poor and persecuted, while it atrophies among the rich and secure."[118] In this sense, the European responsibility of Christians is toward Africa (by the way, it was Europe's founding fathers' idea). It was in the past and it will be so in the future, and this renews us.

There is an underlying idea in Christian communities, in the life and in the faith of European Christians. Actually, it is a proposal sparked by faith, but at the same time very secular: We cannot live for ourselves, for our individual, group, or national interests. Here is the root of that universalism, that permeates Europeans culture. The Gospel opens hearts and minds to a deeper sense of life; it suggests a different orientation; it cultivates a wider vision. It can stimulate Europe to have an extroverted existence: to go out, to project itself, to

---

118. Philip Jenkins, *The Next Christendom: The Coming of Global Christianity* (Oxford: Oxford University Press, 2002), 274.

be a courageous and generous presence in the world. The Gospel can be a vital secret of a liberation from senility and fear. The lives of Christians can affect society, its behavior, and politics. Paul expressed this secret of the Gospel very well: "For Christ's love compels us, because we are convinced that one died for all, and therefore all died. And he died for all, that those who live should no longer live for themselves but for him who died for them and was raised again" (2 Corinthians 5:14–15).

This can be the secret of Europe.

Six

Peace, Fraternity and Dialogue among Religions

After 1989, our world seemed to focus on breaking down walls and overcoming the contrasts and conflicts that had characterized the Cold War. The new century, we might say, started in 1989, when the Berlin Wall, which divided the old German capital, was pulled down: This seemed to represent the end of walls and closed borders. What came down was what Winston Churchill, in a speech in 1945, called the "Iron Curtain", which had divided Europe into two worlds, restricted freedom in the countries in Eastern Europe, and persecuted religious life. In the last decade of the twentieth century, a different world was beginning, in which it seemed that the free market, democracy, and freedom would become victorious and universal. This was no longer the century of the two World Wars, Nazism and fascism, the Holocaust, colonialism, totalitarianisms, and so on.

With this "new world" on the horizon, in which the free market would have a central role as the driving force of change, the public looked absent-mindedly at the question of religion. For many people in this postmodern world, religions represented a universe linked to the past. In Europe, Christianity was becoming weaker and marginalized in society, with the rise of secularism.

The Advocacy of Religions and Pope John Paul II

Pope John Paul II started his pontificate with the cry: "Do not be afraid." He was talking to the believers of Eastern Europe, giving them once more the hope of freedom, but he was also addressing the believers of Western Europe. During the 1980s, Wojtyla had developed a very different vision of religions from the current one that relegated them to the past or obscurantist forces. The Islamic renaissance had taken place: In 1979, Ayatollah Khomeini returned from exile to Iran. He created an Islamic Republic proposing Islam as the basis for a revolution of the oppressed people of the earth. Religions, which by people in the West were considered as realities in decline, were in fact becoming the protagonists of public life, at least in some parts of the world. Several radical and fundamentalist movements were developing in the religious world, and their attitude was highly confrontational.

From 1978, the year he was elected, the Pope saw how Christianity in Poland became a force of hope and resistance against the Soviet communist regime. He revived the Polish people and supported *Solidarnosc*, the trade union and libertarian movement, a process of moral reawakening that brought down the regime, and in some way, undermined the Eastern bloc. In history, little has been said about the decisive role of Pope John Paul II and his Church in the change that took place in 1989.[119] However, Christianity appeared to be the driving force behind this page of history.

In 1986, Pope John Paul II invited the leaders of the world's great religions to Assisi to pray side by side for peace—no longer against each other, as had been the case for thousands of years.[120] Many Catholics were worried that the Pope would put all the religions on the same level, making them all equal. Cardinal Ratzinger was also of this

---

119. See my own: *Giovanni Paolo II. La biografia* (Cinisello Balsamo: San Paolo Edizioni, 2011).
120. Riccardo Burigana, *La pace di Assisi: 27 ottobre 1986. Il dialogo tra le religioni trent'anni dopo* (Milan: Edizioni Terra Santa, 2016).

opinion, but when he was elected Pope, he celebrated the twenty-fifth anniversary of the meeting in Assisi.

Pope John Paul II however, believed in the role of religions in constructing and strengthening peace in a world that was about to overcome the Cold War. They could either encourage more wars or participate in peacemaking. With the end of existing ideologies, religions could in turn become ideologies that sanctified wars or walls.

Pope Wojtyla had a vision, and that was the event that took place in Assisi in 1986. This event completed and surpassed the vision of the Second Vatican Council which, with Nostra Aetate, had opened the dialogue between Catholicism and other religions. The interfaith meeting for peace in 1986 was a concrete and theological turning point: The leaders of Christian Churches and of the other religions in the world made a commitment to living in peace. Peace meant the end of war, but also peaceful coexistence between religious, cultural, and ethnic worlds, to which religions could make a great contribution. In the global world, there were less and less religiously homogenous cities and countries. People of different religions, partly because of immigration, found themselves living in the same places.

From Dialogue to Fraternity

The meeting in Assisi in 1986 gave greater depth to the dialogue between religions, which until then had only taken place between delegations of experts on specific topics. It was basically an academic, theological, spiritual, and cultural dialogue. To what extent could this kind of dialogue engage the faithful? Very little, whereas the event in Assisi was something that really did involve the faithful of various religions. On that unforgettable day, October 27, the atmosphere there was one of a great event of history.

Not only because the leaders of the religions represented different worlds, but because the image of the Pope among the religious leaders, had a contagious effect, and showed the beauty of being together. Seeing those leaders, with their different clothes, close together in peace, expressed the aesthetics of coexistence. It is a beautiful image that is a popular proposal for people, as well as a call to religions to establish coexistence in peace.

Pope John Paul II's final speech in Assisi in 1986 moved me greatly. He said something important that I would like to quote at length:

> There is no peace without a passionate love for peace. There is no peace without an indomitable will to achieve peace. Peace awaits its prophets. Together we have filled our gazes with visions of peace: They release energies for a new language of peace, for new gestures of peace, gestures that will break the fatal chains of divisions inherited from history or generated by modern ideologies. Peace awaits its makers. . . . Peace is a construction site open to all, not only to specialists, savants, and strategists. Peace is a universal responsibility: It passes through a thousand small acts of daily life. Depending on their daily way of living with others, men choose to be for peace or against peace.[121]

Pope Wojtyla saw the beginning of a peace movement that would involve not only the institutions but would bring believers together as brothers—not just specialists

---

121. *Address of John Paul II to the Representatives of the Christian Churches and Ecclesial Communities and of the World Religions,* Basilica of Saint Francis, 27 October 1986, https://www.vatican.va/content/john-paul-ii/en/speeches/1986/october/documents/hf_jp-ii_spe_19861027_prayer-peace-assisi-final.html.

and strategists, but a movement that would impose itself through people's everyday decisions for peace. It sounded like a dream. However, that day in October 1986 we could feel that something profound and historical had taken place. Centuries-old contrasting positions, long distances, structural and theologized indifferences were all about to be overcome. It was the beginning of a fraternity of men and women of different religions in the world.

This fraternity among religions was connected to world peace. Pope John Paul II had taken into consideration what was "discovered" in Assisi: "We have once again discovered that as far as the problem of peace and its realization is concerned, there is something uniting us."[122]

A Unique Event or a Process of Fraternity?

After that "prophetic" (I only use this expression rarely, but it is necessary here) event, there were many attempts to minimize it, even in good faith. There was fear of confusion between religions (in this case, Cardinal Ratzinger), but also the difficulty in understanding that a new fertile field was being found. This is the position of people who are lazy, who consider the work of the Church as belonging to the institution: Becoming part of history and meeting the other is always risky. People started saying that the event in Assisi in 1986 was exceptional and that it could only take place with the Pope. There was in fact an institutional reaction from the Roman Curia to make sure the event would not have a follow-up.

I, on the other hand, with the Community of Sant'Egidio, was convinced that we should continue along that path through meetings among religions. Every year, starting in Rome and later in other cities around the world, we invited

---

122. Ibid.

representatives of different religions to talk about peace and fraternity, but above all to pray. I remember the cold atmosphere of the Curia at the time of the first meeting after the event in Assisi in 1987. However, when Pope John Paul II received us, he said, "You must continue!" He dreamed of a movement of fraternity that would start from the event in Assisi, but he realized that it would be difficult.

The journey has not always been easy over the years, but fraternity between people has increased. It means friendship among people who belong to different religious worlds. The dialogue has turned into something deeper: fraternity and friendship. In the meeting in the spirit of Assisi, held in Rome on October 6 and 7, 2021, Pope Francis said the following: Wojtyla "dreamed of a common journey of believers, starting from the Assisi meeting and advancing toward the future." Pope Francis added:

> Dear friends, we are making that journey, each with his or her own religious identity, to cultivate peace in the name of God and to acknowledge that we are brothers and sisters. Pope John Paul II raised this challenge.... To some this seemed empty optimism. Over the years, however, sharing and forms of dialogue between different religious worlds have increased, thus creating paths to peace. This is the true way forward. If there are those who work to foment division and conflict, we ourselves believe in the importance of journeying together for peace: *with* one another, and never again *against* one another.[123]

---

123. Final Ceremony of the Meeting of Prayer for Peace Organized by the Community of Sant'Egidio: Peoples as Brothers and Sisters, Future Earth. Religions and Cultures in Dialogue. https://www.vatican.va/content/francesco/en/speeches/2021/october/documents/20211007-incontro-preghiera-perlapace.html).

This is a historically correct reconstruction. After the event in Assisi, a process began, and despite difficult phases, it has moved forward to the present situation—a significant legacy for our world.

The Clash between Civilizations and the Crisis of Ecumenical Ideals

I have to be honest and mention some problems. First of all, the will of some people to use religions so as to divide, create conflict, and motivate hate and terror. The terrible attacks of September 11, 2001, on the United States of America marked the beginning of a twenty-first century that was meant to be one of peace and democracy. It was the collapse of the dream of peace that people had after the Berlin Wall came down. In the light of Islamic based terrorism, many people asked us, what good were your meetings, dialogue, fraternity between believers of various religions? What was the point? This question is meaningless. It is like asking, what is the use of praying? I would rather ask, what would the world be like without prayer, fraternity, and dialogue?

The theory of the clash of civilizations began to assert itself. Every civilization had its own religion, so there was also a clash of religions, which appeared to contradict the idea of fraternity and coexistence.[124] The attacks of September 11 seemed to confirm the theory of the clash of civilizations. We were supposed to watch out for people who were "different." It was argued that there was an irreconcilable clash between the Christian and the Islamic world. The

---

124. Samuel P. Huntington, *The Clash of Civilization and the Remaking of World Order* (New York: Simon and Schuster, 1996).

meetings between the religions were described as naïve, whereas clashes were considered reality.

Nobody denies the reality of extremism and terrorism that uses religion for its aggressive ends. How can we respond to this culture of violence? With armies, walls, preventive war...? I am not a pacifist, but the history of the last decades has shown the results of wars conceived in the logic of a clash of civilizations or in an attempt to impose democracy. I will mention only the cases of Afghanistan and Iraq.

Disoriented men and women, on global horizons, put into new situations, living with people of different ethnicities and religions, often immigrants, have felt the need to reaffirm their own identities. More and more borders and walls have gone up, even in Europe. After thirty years, globalization has not produced a united, democratic world, as we were promised, but a world where old suspicions, and the prejudices of yesterday have come back, sometimes even stronger than before.

The great ideals that developed after the wars of the twentieth century and which globalization seemed to bring into being, were being obscured. The great beacons that had illuminated humanity after World War II seemed to be fading: the search for peace, dialogue, ecumenism, the passion for fraternal coexistence, the sense of justice, international cooperation.... They were obscured by the logic of exclusive national interest, contrasting identities, and the acceptance of violence and war.

Pope Francis wrote in *Fratelli tutti*: "In today's world, the sense of belonging to a single human family is fading, and the dream of working together for justice and peace seems an outdated utopia." Has this utopia been buried? Are we living in a world without dreams and visions for a future that also includes others?

War and Peace

Pope Francis said, "One chooses war easily using any type of excuse seemingly humanitarian, defensive, or preventive, even resorting to the manipulation of information. In fact, in past decades all the wars used the pretext of being 'justified'." He then strongly condemned war, based on the Church's historical experience: "Every war leaves our world worse than it was before. War is a failure of politics and of humanity, a shameful capitulation, a stinging defeat before the forces of evil. Let us not remain mired in theoretical discussions but touch the wounded flesh of the victims. Let us . . . look at reality through their eyes and listen with an open heart to the stories they tell. In this way, we will be able to grasp the abyss of evil at the heart of war. Nor will it trouble us to be deemed naïve for choosing peace."[125]

Those who believed in peace and coexistence have been treated as naïve. On the other hand, what has war led us to in these years? Today we are in a highly tense international situation, in a disorderly, divided, conflictual, and confused world. Sometimes it seems as though peace is at risk. After all, with easily available powerful arms, people can carry out terrorist attacks and destabilize whole countries.

Primo Levi, with the strength of someone who survived Auschwitz, always repeated an expression, that is also found in George Santayana (written in many languages on the Dachau monument): "Those who cannot remember the past are condemned to repeat it." We, the sons and daughters of the twentieth century who, if only because of our contact with the previous generations, have known what the horror

---

125. Prayer Meeting for Peace, with Leaders of Christian Churches and World Religions, October 25, 2022. https://www.vatican.va/content/francesco/en/speeches/2022/october/documents/20221025-incontro-pace.html.

of war is like, who have listened to Holocaust survivors, who have seen Europe destroyed, have a responsibility to share the testimony of the horror of war. It shows the precious value of peace. The peace that we Europeans enjoy makes us responsible for passing on the testimonies of the horror of war to the generation born in this century.

In this perspective, I have become convinced that religions are a reserve of hope and action for peace. Monseigneur Rossano, a great builder of interreligious dialogue, said, "We are aware that religion as such is a weak force... but it possesses the force of the spirit which can make it strong, invincible and finally victorious." We know the weakness of religions. We know it in the Catholic Church. However, there is a strength, wrapped in weakness: prayer, fraternity, a responsibility toward others. In 2014, in Antwerp, during the meeting in the spirit of Assisi, I said, "We have continued from 1986 onward, year after year, gathering religious men and women, humanists, to work on the delicate spiritual but tangible frontier between war, religion and peace. We did it believing that war can never be holy, but only peace is."

The Steps Taken by Religions

I am not pessimistic, despite the difficult situation in the contemporary world, the ambiguities of the clash of civilizations, the defense of our ethnic-national identity, and the revival of nationalisms. Despite all this, over the last twenty years, religions have shown that they are a reserve of peace, in a warlike world that has lost its horror of war. In every religious tradition, in different ways, peace is a value. Many years ago, Monseigneur Rossano wrote, "Every religion, when expressed at its best, strives for peace." Even though religions may have been exploited for war, peace is rooted deep down inside them.

In the twenty-first century, religions' awareness of their mission of peace has increased. Dialogue, fraternal meetings, living together (sometimes imposed by necessity) in various urban contexts, has led to greater maturity. In the past, religions and their representatives were often not used to talking with others. Theirs was a monologue that developed in parallel with others. Coexistence has slowly turned every monologue into a dialogue—a dialogue on concrete issues: those regarding an environment in which we live together, issues regarding reconciliation in a context of so much tension, or regarding collaboration.

One episode in the spirit of the event in Assisi is particularly dear to me. In Abidjan, in Ivory Coast, a mosque had been burned down, and the Muslims were going to burn down a church. However, they were stopped by the Catholic priest, the imam and the Protestant parson, who all rushed to prevent it. Then in Lahore, in Pakistan, where the Christian minorities are poor and marginalized, the imam of the great mosque, Massoud, went to a Christian area, and with his authority he prevented violence against the Christians.

Before the pandemic, in 2019, the *Document on Human Fraternity for World Peace and Living Together* was signed. This was an important step. Pope Francis and the Grand Imam of al-Azhar, Tayyb, the highest authority of Sunni Islam, were the most important figures of this event. Tayyb, a Muslim with a spiritual history, has attended meetings for peace in the spirit of Assisi at the initiative of the Community of Sant'Egidio. This document is a platform for Christian-Muslim meetings, but also for other religions. It says:

> History shows that religious extremism, national extremism and also intolerance have produced in the world, be it in the East or West, what might be referred to as signs of a 'third world war being fought piecemeal.' In several parts of the world and in many

tragic circumstances these signs have begun to be painfully apparent....[126]

The problem is living together in fraternity. The document says, "The authentic teachings of religions invite us to remain rooted in the values of peace; to defend the values of mutual understanding, human fraternity, and harmonious coexistence." This document, signed by an important Islamic authority, is strategic for the religious worlds, including the Sunni Muslim world that feels humiliated by the fact that its faith is confused with extremism. It finds in this document an important steppingstone for stating that Islam is not a religion of death and terror. The other religions and the Church of Rome acknowledge this. Moreover, during his journey to Iraq, Pope Francis visited the Grand Ayatollah al-Sistani, the highest authority of the Iraqi Shiite world, in a humble gesture of respect, thus completing his contact with another part of the Muslim world. The relations between the Catholic Church and the Muslim world, at least in their most significant aspects, have improved considerably; in fact, there has been a real breakthrough.

The development of the fraternity between the leaders and the believers of religions is an unequivocal fact. Besides, the dramatic experience of Covid19 brought about a more cooperative conscience among religions. The pandemic was a global event: It showed that it was a challenge to face together. The religious worlds have always been connected to national histories and ethnic realities, but because of the nature of their message, they transcend these realities. They perceive, with their deep instinct and daily contact with

---

126. *A Document on Human Fraternity for World Peace and Living Together*, https://www.vatican.va/content/francesco/en/travels/2019/outside/documents/papa-francesco_20190204_documento-fratellanza-umana.html

the faithful, that the problems of the pandemic and post-pandemic world must be faced together on a universal scale.

The Fraternity of Religions and the Future of the World

In 2021 and 2022, despite the pandemic, two meetings were held in Rome between religious leaders in the spirit of Assisi, and they were attended by Pope Francis, the Orthodox Patriarch of Constantinople, Bartholomew, the Grand Imam of al-Azhar, Tayyb, and other religious leaders, to show that religions do not withdraw into isolation. It was precisely during these meetings that I noticed how these leaders were clearly developing the idea that the pandemic was making us face the world's problems together.

This can make us more optimistic about the future. In some way, as a result of the pandemic, the religious worlds developed a more universal conscience. The Patriarch Bartholomew very lucidly said, "The old world does no longer exist; we have in our hands the possibility to construct a new beginning which must be there for everybody." The president of the European Rabbis, Pinchas Goldsmith, reiterated this point in the sense of interdependence. "If there is one thing that this malicious and treacherous virus has taught the world, it is the total interdependence of the human race. Even if the rich countries vaccinate all their citizens, ignoring the third world, a new mutation coming from it might make their vaccine irrelevant and obsolete. Covid 19 has taught us all humility and vulnerability. Humanity able to reach planet Mars has been humiliated by this invisible and microscopic being...."[127]

---

127. Speech of Pinchas Goldschmidt, President of the Conference of European Rabbis at the International Meeting of Prayer for Peace,

Covid was a lesson in humility for believers who discovered they were in the same boat of humanity as other people. This is a sign of hope. The religions remind us to be aware, that our own behavior is not irrelevant, but it is decisive for our salvation, that of others and that of the earth. Thus, a new world, one that would replace the world that ended with the pandemic, could start with each of us: from me, from us. Martin Buber wrote: "Beginning from ourselves is the only thing that counts ... the point of Archimedes from which I can on my part inspire the world is the transformation of myself." Religions invite us to start from ourselves. It can be an overwhelming wave, a movement of fraternity, as Pope Wojtyla dreamed of in 1986.

After the theory of the clash of civilizations, we moved into a period in which every country often considers itself to be an island, in any case thinking only about itself. Religions remind us of the common destiny of humanity and invite each of us to act accordingly. Fraternity among religions is a valid support for peace, and it is also a way to strengthen living together among different people. In fact, the future is not a clash of civilizations but is living together in a civilized way. This is how Pope Francis ended the interfaith meeting in Rome: "Brother nations, future world. We have a vision ... the world like a shared home, where the brotherhood of nations live. Yes, we dream of sister religions and brother nations! Sister religions that help nations become brothers in peace, peacemaking custodians of creation, our shared home."

This is our dream too.

POPOLI FRATELLI TERRA FUTURA ROME, 6 October 2021, https://preghieraperlapace.santegidio.org/pageID/31365/langID/en/text/3641/Speech-of-Pinchas-Goldschmidt.html

Seven
Sister Churches, Brother Nations

The Origin of a Dream

In his conversations with the Orthodox French theologian Olivier Clément, Athenagoras, the ecumenical Patriarch of Constantinople from 1948 to 1972, used the expression "Sister Churches, Brother Nations." The conversations were published in France in 1969 by the publisher Cerf and came out in several re-editions. In the end, they were collected for Italian readers in a volume called *Umanesimo spirituale* (Spiritual humanism),[128] which I consider one of the greatest texts on spirituality of the twentieth century. The Patriarch was talking with Clément about the value of a mixed society, like that of empires, from a religious and ethnic point of view. The professor pointed out, predicting the future and it was in 1968, how the world was going through two contradictory processes—On the one hand, "the coming of the planetary man, in a story that becomes a global one"; and on the other hand, "maybe to escape the impersonality of the industrial world, every nation clings to its own originality." Today we would talk about globalization, and, paradoxically, of retreating into our identity.

It was the time of the Cold War. The Patriarch, however, was already aware of the intention to unify the world. He predicted a drive toward a global world, countered or maybe

---

128. Athenagoras and Olivier Clément, *Umanesimo spiritual: Dialoghi tra Oriente e Occidente*, Andrea Riccardi, ed. (Cinisello Balsamo: San Paolo, 2013). See also Andrea Riccardi, *Il Professore e il patriarca: Umanesimo spirituale tra nazionalismi e globalizzazione* (Milan: Jaca Book, 2018).

accompanied by reactions concerning identity. We must not forget that in 1968 Marshall McLuhan published *War and Peace in the Global Village*.[129] In the conversation with the professor, the Patriarch said, "We, Christians, should place ourselves at the juncture of these two movements (unification of the world and particularism), in an attempt to harmonize them…" He gets to the heart of the vision: "Sister Churches, Brother Nations: Such should be our example and our message."[130]

The fraternity between Churches is intertwined with the fraternity between people. This message has always struck me in my spiritual and cultural (not personal) meetings with the Patriarch. I went to Istanbul in my early twenties in the summer of 1972, but the Patriarch had died a month earlier. However, I met the Metropolitan Meliton, a great expert in dialogue. In the poor district of Phanar of that time, "a tiny boat, full of the relics of an immense shipwreck," as Clément called it, great dreams were nurtured. Those may be the visions that are missing today because we are in a period in which we often proceed by trial and error and are affected by the ravages of history.

The Patriarch was afraid of an all-technical unification (his expression) or one that might be economic and financial in times of globalization. At Christmas 1968, he said, "Woe, if one day people participate in a union outside the structure and theology of the Church." It would be tragic if Christians did not come together as the world was coming together. This is exactly what has happened though: The world has become globalized but Christian unity is far away, while spiritual globalization, through dialogue, is yet to come. The

---

129. Marshall McLuhan and Quentin Fiore, *War and Peace in the Global Village* (New York: Bantam, 1968).
130. Athenagoras and Clément, *Umanesimo spirituale*, 268.

Patriarch's vision developed when he was a young deacon in Macedonia, during World War I, where bloody battles were fought. His vision of peace grew in the nationalist melting pot of the Balkans, where religion often meant ethnicity.

Angelo Giuseppe Roncalli, the future Pope John XXIII, who was five years older than the Patriarch, was a soldier and military chaplain during World War I. He was as patriotic as the other young people of his generation. However, he was faithful to Benedict XV. He wrote, "War has been and remains evil and whoever has understood the sense of Christ and of his Gospel and the spirit of human and Christian fraternity, will never know how to detest it enough. Neither do we want to be too naïve to expect big things from war...."[131] The following question is also significant: Does one expect too much from war?

These are the observations of a young man who was to go to the Far East, Bulgaria, Greece, and Turkey, as a delegate of the pope, bringing together Orthodox Christians, Jews, and Muslims. Roncalli came back to the West as a nuncio to France and a bishop in Italy. On the other hand, Athenagoras, after experiencing the war in the Balkans and being a bishop on the island of Corfu that was bombed by Mussolini, went West. He lived in the United States for years, until 1948, when he was elected to the ecumenical Patriarchate. Two existential intersecting curves—the Pope who went from the West to the East and the Patriarch who went from the East to the West, in a long-distance dialogue from 1958, the season of the ecumenical spring.

This observation is not mine but is of Father Andrei Scrima, an important figure in ecumenicalism, who by now has almost been forgotten. He was a Romanian monk,

---

131. Marco Roncalli, *Giovanni XXIII: Angelo Giuseppe Roncalli: Una vita nella storia* (Milan: Mondadori, 2006), 121.

a collaborator of Athenagoras. During World War II he was initiated into the practice of the prayer of the heart and then went to India and lived there for years. He was one of the people who built bridges between Athenagoras, Pope John XXIII, and Pope Paul VI. For ecumenism is, perhaps above all, a question of humanity, of friendship, and of fraternity found again after centuries. During that time, hostilities shaped cultures and mentalities, and produced the self-reference and self-sufficiency of Churches and their leaders.

Ecumenism, which developed as an aspiration in the middle of wars and nationalisms, is clear about the link between the fraternity of Christians of different Churches and the peace and cooperation of nations.

Ecumenical Passion: the Rise and Fall of a Unitive Sentiment

The years in which ecumenism developed clearly were those in which the divisions created by the Cold War and by nationalisms were challenged. According to a great visionary, Giorgio La Pira, those years were full of what he called the "unitive tensions." Ecumenism, interreligious dialogue, commitment for peace and disarmament, cooperation between the Global North and the Global South, Third-Worldism, and ecologism were part of it. These were all bridges built over the wall dividing destinies. Some of these tensions find acceptance and an ecclesiological place in the Second Vatican Council.

This Council was the first (pan-European) assembly to transcend the Cold War, with priests from Eastern and Western Europe, but also from the Southern Hemisphere. It was well before the conference for Security and Co-operation in Europe, held in Helsinki in 1975, which was an expression of the cooperation between East and West European countries, committing the signatory states to contribute to European security and to respect human rights.

The presence at the Second Vatican Council of observers from the non-Catholic Churches (some later became leaders of their Churches and protagonists of the dialogue, like the Syriac Patriarch Zhakka) was an absolute novelty in the history of the Councils of the second Christian millennium. According to the leading historian of the Second Vatican Council, Giuseppe Alberigo, this gave the Council an original and unique ecumenical nature compared to the previous Catholic assemblies. Mauro Velati, in a study of the observers, shows how they actively participated in the Council's dynamics, which was against the regulations, in a way representing those who were absent, which prevented the Council from looking at Catholicism only.[132] Besides, from when it was convened, one of the Council's aims was unity, as can be seen from Pope John XXIII's allocution at the Basilica of Saint Paul in 1959, when, with reference to the Second Vatican Council, he spoke of "the search for unity and mercy, for which so many souls yearn all over the world."[133] A rarely quoted passage of the *Unitatis Redintegratio*, the conciliar document on the relations between divided Christians, shows the breadth of the ecumenical task that concerns not only the specialists:

> The attainment of union is the concern of the whole Church, faithful and shepherds alike. This concern

---

132. Cf. Mauro Velati, *Separati ma fratelli. Gli osservatori non cattolici al Vaticano II (1962–1965)* (Bologna: Il Mulino, 2014).
133. *ALLOCUZIONE DEL SANTO PADRE GIOVANNI XXIII CON LA QUALE ANNUNCIA IL SINODO ROMANO, IL CONCILIO ECUMENICO E L'AGGIORNAMENTO DEL CODICE DI DIRITTO CANONICO, Sala capitolare del Monastero di San Paolo, Domenica, 25 gennaio 1959*, https://www.vatican.va/content/john-xxiii/it/speeches/1959/documents/hf_j-xxiii_spe_19590125_annuncio.html

extends to everyone, according to his talent, whether it be exercised in his daily Christian life or in his theological and historical research. This concern itself reveals already to some extent the bond of brotherhood between all Christians and it helps toward that full and perfect unity which God in His kindness wills.[134]

If the vision, as God's plan to be realized, means full and perfect unity, there already is a deep bond, albeit in the division, beginning with baptism, as the theological dialogue highlights. This bond compels everyone to reestablish unity in everyday life as well as in historical-theological studies. People have their role in ecumenism. Because of that deep instinct that exists in people, the ecumenical and interreligious dialogue means we have to look beyond our fences, toward the awareness of the need for dialogue that was matured in the great Second Vatican Council.

Ecumenical passion, which has been increasing since the 1960s, moves along these lines, in which not only theological dialogue has its place, but also the network of meetings and connections. It shows how we can no longer be alone, "never without the other," as Michel de Certaeau used to say.[135] Looking for unity together was already in itself a unifying factor among Christians. I like to remember the words spoken by Athenagoras in 1961 to some students of the Roman high school "Virgilio," where the Community of Sant'Egidio started a few years later: "You come from a Church with which we have almost everything in common . . . the same Lord, the same Gospel, the same faith. The martyrs of the Colosseum

---

134. *Decree on Ecumenism, Unitatis Redintegratio*, Par. 5, 1964 https://www.vatican.va/archive/hist_councils/ii_vatican_council/documents/vat-ii_decree_19641121_unitatis-redintegratio_en.html).
135. Michel de Certeau, *Mai senza l'altro. Viaggio nella differenza* (Magnano: Edizione Qiqajon, 2007).

are common to us.... If there are differences that came later, we must not forget that, above and beyond them, there is the spirit of charity...."[136]

At that time, the ecumenical meetings resounded among people, as did the visit of Athenagoras in Rome in 1968. The ecumenical tension was set against the backdrop of strong unifying tensions that aimed to overcome polarization and walls. There is a coincidence with the worldwide thaw in the climate of the Cold War and with the emergence of a pluralistic, different world compared to the rigid system of the two empires.

The meeting in Jerusalem in January 1964 between Pope Paul VI and Athenagoras had a symbolic value, the scope of which went beyond the ecclesiastic circles and introduced the figure of the Patriarch and his successors in the Catholic imagination as internal and no longer extraneous. Athenagoras' dream was to reach the common chalice, as he said, and Pope Paul VI was not opposed. It did not happen, for complex reasons, including the opposition of Catholic ecumenists, who feared controversy among the Orthodox Christians.[137] A decade later ecumenical dialogues, prepared between 1976 and 1978 by the Joint International Commission for Theological Dialogue between the Catholic Church and the Orthodox Church began.

Starting in the 1980s, the ecumenists, maybe in rather a romantic vision of unity, began talking about a cooling off of the ecumenical passion that clashed with the rigidity of the structures and doctrines of the Church. After the spring of the 1960s, the expression "ecumenical winter" was spreading, also with reference to relations between Catholics and

---

136. Testimony given to the author.
137. Alberto Melloni, *Tempus visitationis: L'intercomunione inaccaduta fra Roma e Costantinopoli* (Bologna: Il Mulino, 2019).

Evangelicals. The Catholic ecumenists complained about Rome's lack of foresight. I remember among others, Father Pierre Duprey, who did so much to advance the dialogue. Those who knew about the excommunications and coldness of yesterday, however, cannot fail to see the progress made in respect, in meetings, in agreement. However, we could not go any further.

The Crisis of Ecumenism

After 1989, the story did not end, as some people predicted, but it whirled into action again.[138] Nations, having survived the iciness of the Soviet Union, came back onto the international scene. History, forcefully, even devastatingly, became part of ecumenical issues. I will mention a few: For instance, the question of the Greek-Catholic Ukrainians, who in 1946 were forcefully incorporated into the Russian Church by the Synod of Lviv, during the period of the Soviet Union, and its consequent effects on the difficult Catholic-Russian relations, but also the accusations of Catholic proselytism on the Orthodox side. Another issue involved the end of Yugoslavia, with the Catholic-Orthodox polarization related to the war between Croatia and Serbia. Then the crisis of the celebration of the Pan-Orthodox Council in 2016, a dream of the Patriarch Bartholomew inspired by Athenagoras (the preparations started in the 1960s). The celebration of that Council was marred by the absence of the Russians, Antiochians, Bulgarians, and Georgians. This was followed by the recognition of the Ukrainian Orthodox Church by Constantinople in 2018 and the response of the Moscow Patriarch with the breaking of communion. Some of the Orthodox Ukrainians left the Russian jurisdiction in a Ukraine that was shattered, not

---

138. Cf. Fukuyama, *The End of History*.

only in terms of religion. Regarding Ukraine, one might say, "enemy governments, hostile Churches."

In the dramatic Ukrainian war, after the Russian attack on Kiev, we saw the resurgence of the ideological weapons of religious confrontation, stored in the cellars of the Churches. It was not just a question of a crisis within the Orthodox world, but of a drama of ecumenical significance. By now a bilateral Catholic-Orthodox dialogue was no longer possible, due to the division within the Orthodox side. The ecumenical crisis today is accompanied by the breakdown of so many unitive tensions, *in primis*, peace.

The big, boundless, invasive global world seems to frighten people. They look for refuge in limited perimeters, afraid of the other. They cling to their own identity, opposing it to that of others. It also happens among Catholics in Eastern Europe with respect to nearby countries or refugees, who are perceived as invaders. The Orthodox Bishop of Albania, Anastasios, a close friend since the end of communism and the rebirth of the Albanian Church, said, "The opposite of peace is not war, but selfishness." Selfishness that is personal, ecclesiastical, ethnic, and national.

Ecumenism undoubtedly has limitations. It has concentrated mainly on theological dialogue and has not sufficiently taken people's feelings into account. An "enlightenment" limitation in the belief that doctrinal agreement could lead to unity, has driven Christians away.

Athenagoras said, "Truly theological dialogue should arise naturally within the dialogue of love, within that mystery of the Church which in its fundaments, is common to us. Alongside our work we should all surrender to the Holy Spirit, asking for the intercession of our shared martyrs, priests and saints...."[139]

---

139. Athenagoras and Clément, *Umanesimo spirituale*, 491.

The further we move away from the Council, despite achieving significant gains, the more the method of meeting each other begins to correspond excessively to that used in international organizations or diplomacies—basically, to negotiations or talks between representatives. These systems are characteristic of the Western, Catholic-Lay-Protestant mentality, which has shaped international organizations and countries. They correspond to a somewhat Enlightenment view, as though ideas, taken in an abstract sense, were the engine of history, considered almost separately from men. For the Slavic world, for example, separating the person from the truth of which he is the bearer, is not possible. I am not referring to theological work as an in-depth search for agreement in the language of faith, knowledge of history.... I am talking about a way of negotiating among Churches, attempted on one hand through the model of international organizations and on the other hand through an Enlightenment ideological approach. It may have been a necessary step, but it is not enough.

Basically, ecumenism is not only played out between Churches, resembling disembodied entities, but between Christians belonging to different worlds and civilizations. Without indulging in Huntington's theory, it must be recognized that the conflicts between civilizations deeply involve the Churches. There are ecumenical problems concerning civilizations, political, social, and economic problems of the past and of the present.

Churches are part of civilization, and they have a memory, which sometimes becomes an epic that is shared by the whole of society. Memory and prejudice are sometimes the way through which we get to know each other, knowing and having respect for the other by involving not only hierarchies but also people and populations. An Italian mystic, Giovanni Vannucci, said: "One needs to know in order to love more."[140]

Christians in a Non-ecumenical History

The history of our global century has not been ecumenical. Just think of the theory of the clash of civilizations, in which religion plays an identifying role, which seems to be confirmed by the tragic attacks of September 11, 2001. Ours is not a peaceful present; on the contrary, it shows old walls, old nationalistic passions, against a backdrop of an interconnected and financially unified world, which has at its disposal sophisticated and destructive weapons and a network of information that also conveys hatred and prejudice. History has spread over relationships between Christians since they are part of it.

The pursuit of Christian unity is not a fad, or a debt paid to a politically correct cosmopolitan spirit, but is rooted in a commandment of the Lord, too long disregarded, while preaching the observance of other commandments. We are reminded of the words of Jesus: "Woe unto you, scribes and Pharisees, hypocrites! for ye pay tithe of mint and anise and cummin, and have omitted the weightier matters of the law, judgment, mercy, and faith" (Matthew 23:23).

We must experience the differences and even the clashes within the structure of peace and unity that fundamentally characterizes Christians. Healing divisions begins by immediately walking toward unity, as what happened in the Gospel to the royal official who prayed to Jesus for his sick son: "'Go,' Jesus replied, 'your son will live.' The man took Jesus at his word and departed" (John 4:50).

---

140. Cf. Massimo Orlandi, *Giovanni Vannucci custode della luce* (Rome: Edizioni Romena, 2005).

Today, when unity as a fundamental characteristic of Christianity appears obscured, division does not cause a scandal. On the contrary, it legitimizes the neo-Evangelist or neo-Pentecostal movement (well over half a billion people) which, particularly in some countries, takes on a fragmentary and competitive character in the market of religions. Moreover, today there is a shocking extent of polarization within the Catholic Church, like living apart together. According to the Rabbi Jonathan Sacks, the process of the fragmentation of our world, the change in the cultural climate, has led to an ego-oriented society. The lack of unity brings us back to the question of peace. The divisions between Christians are connected to those between people.

Christians, however, by the very nature of their faith, cannot let themselves be overwhelmed by divisive processes. The search for unity is not an opportunity but is a destiny, the will of the Lord. The seeds of unity are everywhere in Churches. Today, among Christians of various denominations, we speak as brothers. There are intense collaborations on many levels. Sometimes the seeds ripen thanks to events that suggest new visions. I remember the meeting in Assisi, initiated by John Paul II. In the icon of Assisi 1986 there are simple but basic insights for ecumenical relations, interreligious dialogue, the contribution of religions to peace. Interreligious dialogue finds an important shelter in peace and prayer. Moreover, it is precisely in the image of Assisi, full of theological meaning, but not very well explored, that we understand how little divides Christians.

During the prayer for peace in Assisi a woman said to me, "What little difference there is between Christians," as she watched them walking among Buddhists, Jews, and Muslims. Christians divided in the face of a pluralistic world. It is the case of the Christians in the Middle East, confronted with the Muslim majority. How little divides them and how much unites them! The Community of Sant'Egidio wanted the Assisi journey to continue every year in various cities throughout the world—common prayer and a tight network of dialogue around it.

I would like to recall, in particular, a meeting promoted by Sant'Egidio in Bucharest, in 1988. It was a high-profile Pan-Orthodox meeting with patriarchs and primates, in the context of a dialogue between Christians and people of other religions, as pointed out by Hazim, the Orthodox Patriarch of Antioch. The meeting was influenced by the pain caused by the issue between Orthodox and Greek-Catholics in Romania and the debate on the return of the Greek-Catholic Churches, which came into the possession of the Patriarchate during the communist regime. That meeting was not a negotiation but an event of cooperation and unity involving the people. From the very first day, when Patriarch Teoctist presided over the Latin liturgy in the Catholic Cathedral, it appeared evident that there had been a shift from the ritual reception to a participatory reception at the level of the people.

The people were important because they clearly manifested their willingness to find an agreement. This was seen in the enthusiastic reception of the gestures of understanding, above all, in the final interfaith event in the presence of several thousands of people. The people were the players in a process of reconciliation. The Patriarch Athenagoras said, "The theologians have their word, but the people have their word too. It is something profoundly right in the instinct of God's people." The meeting in Bucharest opened the way for Pope John Paul II's visit in 1999, the first visit to an Orthodox country. I remember Wojtyla's dream of being able to take communion in the Orthodox liturgy. With his spiritual instinct he was not forgetting the people when after the liturgy, he shouted "*Unitate, Unitate!*"

The spirit of Assisi is a vision of a global world, almost a globalization of the spirit through the dimension of prayer and dialogue, to work on in this non-ecumenical present of ours. I cannot forget, in a time of fractures, the prayer in Bari in 2018, promoted by Pope Francis, who invited the Christian primates for the Middle East. It followed the impressive pilgrimage in 2017 of St. Nicholas's relics to Russia, in which over two million Russians joined in veneration.

I had a part in planning the initiative in Bari and I remember Pope Francis's enthusiasm in meeting the primates and in the discussion around a table in the Basilica of St. Nicholas. A great sign of hope! I would have liked to talk about the spirit of Bari, unfortunately not picked up much in this difficult period, but one on which to meditate and work.

In this period, perhaps the boldness of the ecclesial players who take the initiative of an ecumenical way should be encouraged, in order to inspire the rebirth of the passion for meeting, the belief that when we pray together, the designs of the divider collapse, as Ignatius of Antioch said.

Local Churches, individuals, ecclesial realities... we all have to go back and experience the scandal of the division and feel the need to unite. This fragmenting world of ours needs a prophecy of unity, which is an alternative vision to relationships of force, of power, of economic interests. Such is fraternity among Christians, which brings peoples close together. Fraternity among the Churches must create a history, a climate, a reality, that "ecumenical civilization" of which Patriarch Bartholomew spoke, the civilization of living together. Perhaps the task of Christian ecumenism is also to make peoples enthusiastic again about the sense of a common destiny, unity, freeing them from the protective covering of mutual fear.

Cardinal Franz Koenig, who crossed the "Iron Curtain" and experienced the coming closer together of Churches, talked about ecumenism as one of the greatest factors in the Second Vatican Council. "The action of the Spirit was clearly visible here. From there we conclude that problems, seemingly insoluble, faced with trust, honest intention, and unlimited confidence in the will of God, find a way out.... Nothing is impossible, in fact nothing is impossible for God."[141]

The spirit of the Council nourishes the "naïve" enthusiasm of the meeting, so we even believe the impossible. It is a challenge: to live in peace and unity even in times of division and war, in the belief that nobody will be able to deprive us of an ideal that gives hope to the world.

---

141. Franz Koenig, *Where is the Church Heading?* (Slough, MN: St. Paul Publications, 1986).

Eight

"How Could You Be My Enemy?"

The Drama of World War I

How does Christianity react in the face of the great crisis generated by a world war? A world war is a *novum* in the history of humanity, as Pope Benedict XV perceived very well.[142] A war between European countries that becomes a world war. In World War I plenty of enthusiastic Christians and Catholics fought for the national cause. Don Primo Mazzolari, a reflective priest and nationally prominent parish priest, an important figure for twentieth-century Italian Catholicism, was interviewed with D'Annunzio, Giovanni Papini, and reformist socialists like Cesare Battisti. He said, "The Lord is with those of us who fight for the just cause."[143] There was the idea that in war people's hearts were purified by sacrifice, while pacifism seemed to Mazzolari a choice of laziness.[144] Lodovico Montini, Pope Paul VI's brother, told me many years ago, "In war they saw how Catholic we Italians are." Mazzolari asked to be enlisted as a military chaplain.

Young Italian Catholics wanted to show that they were Italian, sharing national aspirations. This was not the position of Pope Benedict XV, the Pope of the "useless slaughter." In France, it was the period of the *Union Sacrée*, when

---

142. Cf. Alberto Melloni, *Benedict XV: A Pope in the World of the Useless Slaughter (1914–1918)*, 2 vols. Giovanni Cavagnini, Giulia Grossi, and Pietro Parolin, eds. (Turnhout, Belgium: Brepols, 2020).
143. Stefano Albertini, *Don Primo Mazzolari e il fascismo (1921–1943)* (Bozzolo: Fondazione Don Primo Mazzolari, 1988), 14.
144. Giorgio Vecchio, "L'eredità di don Primo Mazzolari," *Aggiornamenti Sociali,* April 2009. 291–301, 300.

Poincaré's government softened the anticlerical measures, suspended those against religious congregations, and for the first time in the Third Republic, welcomed a Catholic as a minister. The Pope's position on the war was not accepted by many Catholics, who were patriots enthusiastic about the war.

Enthusiasm for the war—and nationalism—was tempered by the harsh realities of those confronting it daily and by its persistence. However, several priests, in particular military chaplains, held onto their nationalist points of view, and in 1922 found themselves supporting fascism and then its military exploits, such as the war in Ethiopia. The Dominican Reginaldo Giuliani, a military chaplain in World War I, was in Fiume with D'Annunzio (where he blessed the dagger given to the commander by women of Fiume). He became the chaplain of the Black Shirts, wrote the Victories of God, and accompanied the fascist expedition in Ethiopia, where he died.[145]

However, Father Primo, a sincere Christian, an impetuous, generous, and intellectually honest man, completely changed his mind about war. As a veteran, he felt shaken and drained by doubt; he was confused. He saw suffering and priests leaving the ministry. So, he said, "The war is not a parade. There... hundreds and thousands died. Those were youngsters, who with a desperate calm asked for a reason to be able to close their eyes in peace. I saw the world, not the worlds of our handbooks... You should have seen us after a week in Carso or Piave: the color of earth, dirty, ragged, flea-bitten, with eyes full of death."

These experiences developed the priest's awareness of the value of peace (Pope John XXIII, in his only meeting with

---

145. Antonio Spinosa, *D'Annunzio: Il poeta armato* (Milano: Mondadori, 1987), 170.

him, called him "the trumpet of the Holy Spirit in the area of Mantua"). In the aftermath of World War II and in the climate of the Cold War, he was committed to peace in a way that worried Pope Pius XIII's Vatican. Mazzolari's journey is typical of many believers, priests, and pastors faced with the drama of war.

It is worth remembering that Angelo Giuseppe Roncalli, the future Pope John XXIII, author of the great and well-known encyclical on peace, *Pacem in terris*, was a soldier and a military chaplain, with the enthusiasm of the young people of his generation. However, he was faithful to the Pope and stated that Pope Benedict XV's note on the "useless slaughter" was in line with the Italian people's deep soul: "War has been and remains a most grievous evil, and those who have understood the sense of Christ and his Gospel and the spirit of human and Christian brotherhood will never know how to sufficiently detest it. Nor do we want to be too naïve to expect great things from war."[146]

Later Monsignor Roncalli, the apostolic delegate to Turkey, followed the outbreak of World War II with great concern and, meditating on Psalm 50, wrote in the *Giornale dell'anima*: "Free me of blood, Oh Lord, Lord my salvation, free us from war and nationalism!" For him, the aspiration for the peace of nations had a foundation: "The savior Jesus, who died for all the nations, without distinction of race or blood, became the first brother of the new family of man...."[147] The pain of the war marks the development of the spiritual humanism of many Christians, not only Catholics, in Europe.

---

146. Marco Roncalli, *Giovanni XXIII. Angelo Giuseppe Roncalli. Una vita nella storia* (Milan: Mondadori 2006), 121.
147. Angelo Giuseppe Roncalli (John XXIII) *Il Giornale dell'anima e altri scritti di pieta* (Rome: Edizioni di Storia e Letteratura, 1975) 282.

There was so much Catholic disaffection toward war, which grew out of the painful experience of World War I and which remains fixed in the memory. (It is from this discontent that the Italian fascist police emerged.) However, Pope Benedict XV's position was coherent during and after the war. The papacy, especially in the twentieth century (but already in the nineteenth century), took a clear and eloquent stance for peace to the heart of the wounds of Europe and the world. And this had implications for Catholics. For the Catholic Church, an international gathering of people that has only one supranational authority, a world war is a morally and structurally impossible situation. (Here we understand the position of the popes post 1870. who have no intention to let the Holy See fall again under the sovereignty of a state, even if offered guarantees and laws regulating the relations between the Italian government and the Holy See.)

The Pope, Peace, and Peace Movements

In 1920, Pope Benedict XV issued an encyclical, *Pacem, Dei munus*, the first one on peace, which came long before Pope John XXIII's *Pacem in terris*, published in 1963. The Pope's main message was that peace must be created with the agreement of people within a just international order. He said, "society would incur the risk of great loss if, while peace is signed, latent hostility and enmity were to continue among the nations." He continued:

> All that We have said here to individuals about the duty of charity We wish to say also to the peoples who have been delivered from the burden of a long war, in order that, when every cause of disagreement has been, as far as possible, removed, and without prejudice to the rights of justice, they may resume friendly relations among themselves. The Gospel has

not one law of charity for individuals, and another for States and nations….The war being now over, people seem called to a general reconciliation not only from motives of charity, but from necessity; the nations are naturally drawn together by the need they have of one another, and by the bond of mutual good will….[148]

It was recognized here how peoples and states had a personality and a subjectivity: Their relationships were to be understood in terms of a "family of nations"; the Pope used this expression, one that comes back into the terminology and thought of the Holy See up to recent times. Here the problem was the Holy See's attitude to the hoped for "Society of Nations," which came into being at the suggestion of the president of the United States, Woodrow Wilson, and which later became the League of Nations.[149] There was a shift from the cautious but sincere favor of Pope Benedict XV (who died in 1922) toward this institution, to an increasingly perplexed attitude of Pope Pius XI, who pointed out that the League of Nations lacked the universalist contribution that only the Church could offer.

After World War I, Catholic pacifism, which indicated the development of a humanism, came into being. It started looking at the world in a global way, precisely from the experience of that war. The first years after World War I were full of Catholic pacifist initiatives, though sometimes short-lived: the international Catholic League, promoted by Alphonse

---

148. Benedict XV, Encyclical, *Pacem, Dei Munus Pulcherrimum*, Given at St. Peter's, Rome, on May 23, 1920, the Feast of Pentecost. Pacem, Dei Munus Pulcherrimum (May 23, 1920) | BENEDICT XV (vatican.va)

149. Cf. Americo Miranda, *Santa Sede e Società delle Nazioni. Benedetto XV, Pio XI e il nuovo internazionalismo cattolico* (Rome: Studium, 2013).

Steger, to coordinate relationships between Catholics in the various countries to stimulate international cooperation; the *Katholiker bund* of the Austrian Father Metzger, who wanted to develop a movement of peace and solidarity with the people affected by the war in the German world; the World Esperanto Congress founded in the Hague in 1920; the *Union Catholique d'Etudes Internationales*, which aimed to promote the study of international law and the presence of Catholics in the League of Nations; Pax Romana founded in 1921 which aimed to involve students from twelve European countries. In 1921, Father Sturzo and Marc Sagnier (founder of an international *Ligue des Socieétés catholiques pour la paix*) held two congresses, which aimed to uniform the Italian and French Catholics' political visions. Finally, Cardinal Mercier, an important player in ecumenical talks with Anglicans but not exclusively, promoted the *Union internationale d'études sociales*, in which social studies were combined with internationalism.

Apart from this rather dry list, we should notice the general characteristic that brings these initiatives together—the support for the entry of Catholics in the League of Nations and for the elaboration of the culture of peace through international law.

A limitation, only overcome in some cases, was to remain within the Catholic world and not involve Christians of all dominations (not easy in a period of great distance between Churches). It is important to point out that Pope Benedict XV encouraged, although cautiously, contact with non-Catholics. However, as Geardóid Barry wrote, the Pope "presided a sort of Catholic internationalist movement after the war . . . "[150] He understood, in the midst of the loneli-

---

150. Gearóid Barry, in: *Benedict XV: A Pope in the World of the Useless Slaughter* (Turnhout, Belgium: Brepols, 2020), Vol. 1, 319–335.

ness of World War I, how the Holy See could not remain isolated in its diplomatic action, but that it had to connect with Catholic players working for peace. This approach was no longer pursued during Pius XI's pontificate.

In the wake of this vision of peace there was the reflection of Father Sturzo, who was not only the founder of the Italian People's Party but also a great sociologist and scholar of international affairs. He was in favor of Italy's intervention in the war but soon had second thoughts and directed his attention toward action against the war. At the end of the 1930s, he said, "I am not and have never been a pacifist in the current sense of the word." However, as Agostino Giovagnoli pointed out, Sturzo elaborated a courageous vision of a path toward the abolition of war as an instrument to resolve conflict, even if it was a question of a "just war" (and he denied that for Christians there were any legitimate wars).[151]

Realism, according to Sturzo, is not vague pacifist utopianism: "One has to have faith that . . . war as a legal means of protection of rights should be abolished, just like polygamy, slavery, serfdom and the family vendetta."[152] In fact, today "war has become so extended politically and technically that it has become an instrument out of proportion in defense of every legal right, and there is so much evil which affects not only the soldiers but the whole world...."[153]

---

151. Agostino Giovagnoli, "Luigi Sturzo e l'abolizione della guerra alla fine degli anni Venti," in *Universalità e cultura nel pensiero di Luigi Sturzo* (Soveria Mannelli: Rubettino Editore, 2001), 425–442.
152. Luigi Sturzo, *Nazionalismo e internazionalismo* (Bologna: Zanichelli, 1971) 184. See in English, Luigi Sturzo, *Nationalism and Internationalism* (New York: Roy Publishers, 2006).
153. Ibid., 183.

Popular Piety and Humanism of the Poor

I would like to underline how the rejection of war does not only belong to the learned or hierarchical figures in Catholicism but is deeply connected to the religious sentiment of the people, as seen in popular piety. We should bear in mind that the apparition of Our Lady of Fatima occurred in 1917. Sister Lucia, one of the young visionaries, narrated in her fourth memoir that she saw Our Lady, who said to her, "Continue to recite the rosary in honor of Our Lady of the Rosary in order to achieve peace in the world and the end of the war because only She can help."[154] Our Lady is presented as the "queen of peace" who responds to people's thirst for peace. Her message to the visionaries is as follows:

> if one listens to my requests then the Russians will convert and there will be peace, otherwise Russia will spread its mistakes around the world, causing wars and persecutions of the Church. The good people will be martyred, the Holy Father will suffer badly because several nations will be annihilated. Finally, my Immaculate Heart will triumph. The Holy Father will consecrate Russia to me, which will be converted, and a certain period of peace will be granted to the world.

This devotion is an answer, not direct but with clear content, to war propaganda. Pope Pius XII often referred to the Marian cult in relation to peace. It was also found after World War II, during the Cold War, and after 1989. Among the hundreds of examples that could be remembered, I will only mention the devotion to Our Lady of Divine Love, who

---

154. Lucia (suor) *Lucia racconta Fatima. Memorie, lettere e documenti di Suor Lucia*, ed. Antonio M. Martins, translated by R. Baraglia and E. Demarchi (Brescia: Queriniana, 1977), 121.

is said to have protected Rome during the hard months of the German occupation and in the hours of its liberation. She was taken to the Church of St Ignatius and venerated by Pope Pius XII, who thanked her for her protection.[155] In more recent times, in 1982, in Kebeho in Rwanda, Our Lady appeared to six girls and a boy. Among other things, violent scenes of war were seen, which were later connected to the Rwandan genocide of 1994.[156] Mary's apparitions in Medjugorje in the 1980s were connected to the violent events that took place in Bosnia-Herzegovina. One of her messages states, "I present myself here as the queen of peace to tell everyone that peace is necessary for the salvation of the world."[157]

During the twentieth century, the link between popular devotion to Mary, considered the "queen of peace," and people's aspirations for peace deepened among public opinion. It gradually widened and became nationalized, even within mass authoritarian regimes. In Italy, during World War II, popular piety took charge of ending the war. It came from the wounded humanity of the "poor," amid the hardships of life and the news of the fighting, in which their relatives were involved. In 1941, a person trusted by the police reported a crowded procession in a small town in Apulia that was crushed by misery and whose young men were at war: "At the end of the procession the crowd entered the church, with the usual scenes of shouting and invocations, typical of these country people. The predominant theme of the manifesta-

---

155. Cf. Nicola Tommasini, *Il Divino amore. Storia tradizione pietà popolare* (Rome: Madonna del Divino Amore, 2003).
156. Cf. Saverio Gaeta, *Kibeho. La Madre del Verbo e il genocidio africano* (Cinisello Balsamo: San Paolo Edizioni, 2018).
157. *Tutti i messaggi di Medjugorje 30 anni con la regina della pace*, ed. Diego Manetti (Casale Monferrato: Piemme, 2011), 82.

tion—the end of the war. During the whole evening— they did not talk of anything else, or invoke anything else"[158]

Peace, Protestantism, and Christian Unity

A strong peace movement developed in the non-Catholic Christian world during World War I. Alberto Schweitzer, a German citizen, originally a parson from Alsace, decided to devote himself to caring for the sick in Lambaréné, in Gabon. He was a missionary physician in Africa for many years.[159] World War I surprised him while he was in Gabon: He was banned from practicing medicine and as he was German, was taken to prison in France. During this period, he wrote important texts, collected under the title *Psycopatologie du nationalism*,[160] in which he noted the failure of "patriotic religion" and invited people to think of war as a "catastrophe." This original figure of a Protestant parson, physician, musician, missionary, and theologian, represented well the Evangelical sensitivity affected by the drama of World War I. He worked for peace until his death in 1965 (in 1952 he received the Nobel Prize for this commitment to peace and for his fight against nuclear weapons).

He was not an Isolated figure. He was supported in his work in Africa by Nathan Söderblom, the Archbishop of Uppsala, who embodied the Christian and Lutheran reaction to the war with a resourcefulness that made him an international point of reference. He was supported by Sweden, which was not involved in the conflict, and com-

---

158. Francesco Malgeri, *La Chiesa italiana e la guerra (1940–1945)* (Rome: Studium, 1980), 97.
159. Pierre Lassus, *Albert Schweitzer 1875–1965* (Paris: Albin Michel, 1995).
160. Albert Schweitzer, *Psychopathologie du nationalisme* (Paris-Orbey: Arfuyen, 2016).

bined his aspiration for Christian unity with that of peace. This was an ecumenical and pacifist issue, not embraced by the Holy See under Pope Benedict XV, despite his being sensitive to non-Catholics, and it was definitively closed with Pope Pius XI. In the Protestant world, on the other hand, ecumenical work, combined with an examination of social problems and peace, developed precisely after World War I.

On 1 August 1914, the World Alliance for International Friendship through the Churches was founded: It held a congress in 1919 during which, encouraged by Archbishop Söderblom, a Movement for Practical Christianity ("Life and Work") was created in order to prepare a world conference of the Churches, which aimed to discuss issues regarding social ethics, including peace. The conference was held in Stockholm in 1925, in the presence of representatives from many Christian Churches, except the Catholic Church. The invitation to the conference stated, "The burning social problems and tensions between the nations show how serious and urgent it is for us Christians ... to see clearly the duty of the Church in the life of people and of nations...."[161]

Söderblom had already made a plea for peace in 1941, indicating the only way in which nationalism was acceptable to Christians: "Patriotism is to be borne in the Praise of God who commands: love your enemies. Then and only then is it baptized and sanctified."[162] The Archbishop was a leading figure in the peace movement. Among other things, he exerted a strong spiritual influence on a young man who

---

161. Raymund Kottje and Bernd Moeller, eds., *Storia ecumenica della Chiesa* (Brescia: Queriniana, 1980), 347–448.
162. Bengt Sundkler, *Nathan Söderblom: His Life and Work* (Cambridge, UK: Lutterworth Press,1968), 162.

spent time with his family, Dag Hammarskjöld, a future Secretary General of the UN who died in 1961 in a plane crash while working to resolve the crisis in Congo.[163] In 1917, he proposed a conference of Protestant Church leaders from neutral countries, like Switzerland, Sweden, Holland, Denmark, and Norway. For him, "the unity of Christians [is] in Christ above the world and above nations."[164] The archbishop's dream came true in Uppsala in 1918 when he succeeded in bringing together not only Protestants but also Orthodox Christians, including Exarch Stefan of Bulgaria.

In this coming together of Christians on an ethical-practical basis, the issue of peace was decisive. We can understand how, for the Catholics, it was difficult to approach ecumenism from a point of view of peace, because of the prevalence of a theological-truthful vision (which was later also found in the ecumenical dialogue itself). Archbishop Söderblom said: "doctrine separates, service unites."[165]

I will not explain here how this movement gradually merged with the "Faith and Constitution" movement that was more focused on the problems of confession, ministries, and sacraments, preparing the way for the future ecumenical Council of Churches, whose first meeting was held in Amsterdam. It was difficult for Germany to participate in the ecumenical movement due to their defeat in World War I. After 1933, with Nazism, it became impossible for political reasons and because of the Nazification of a large part of the Evangelical world (despite the resistance of Bonhoeffer's Confessing Church).

---

163. Cf. Franco Giampiccoli, *Dag Hammarskjöld. Un credente alla guida dell'ONU* (Turin: Claudiana, 2005).
164. Ibid., 201.
165. Erwin Fahlbusch, Jan Milic Lochman, John Mbiti, and Jaroslav Pelikan, eds., *The Encyclopedia of Christianity*, Vol. 5 (Grand Rapids, MI: Wm. B. Eerdmans Publishing, 2008) 5.

Peace and Christian Unity

The Orthodox Christians, on the other hand, were also limited by the national horizon. The Churches had won autocephaly from Constantinople by tying themselves to national revival processes in the Balkans. Significantly, however, after World War I, a discussion on ecumenical and peace issues started. Willem Visser't Hooft, a young Dutch theologian, who became the Secretary of the Ecumenical Council of Churches in 1938, visited the Orthodox Metropolitan of Corfu, Athenagoras, who had already taken part in some ecumenical meetings, for instance the YMCA conference in Helsinki (and was on the executive board with Söderblom). He was very impressed by the Metropolitan, who in 1948 became the ecumenical Patriarch of Constantinople, the man who embraced Pope Paul VI in Jerusalem in 1964.[166] (The Pope told him, "Isn't unity Christ's wish? ... In the end doesn't world peace depend on the conditions of unity of Christ's disciples?")[167]

The original theme, of which Athenagoras was perhaps the most distinguished advocate, is the connection between the unity of Christians and peace or, if you will, the responsibility of divisions among Christians in the face of war. In fact, it was in Constantinople that an encyclical letter written by Patriarch Joachim III, in 1902, on the problem of the closer relationship of Churches, was addressed to all Christians. In 1920, another encyclical, *Unto the Churches of Christ Everywhere*, sent out from the same See, proposed a kind of League of Nations among the Churches. Patriarch Meletios, first Archbishop of Athens, then Patriarch of Constantinople,

---

166. Cf. Valeria Martano, *Athenagoras, il patriarca (1886–1972): Un cristiano fra crisi della coabitazione e utopia ecumenica* (Bologna: Il Mulino, 1996).
167. Ibid., 74.

and finally of Alexandria, had such strong links with the Anglo-Saxon world that he was considered to have close ties with freemasonry. These irenic and ecumenical initiatives were not appreciated by many Orthodox Christians, especially the monks, who defended the preservation and model of the Orthodox State. Not everywhere however, In Bulgaria, Exarch Stefan, a friend of the apostolic delegate Roncalli, a defender of the Jews, participated in this movement.

The big question in the Orthodox world was how to come to terms with history. And history meant, in its most dramatic moments, war and the divisions of the world. During the Soviet regime, the Russian Patriarch, Alexis reiterated, "Even if everything around us changes, we have to remain as we were centuries ago. May our immutability, impossibility to conform to the spirit of the time, be a symbol of the eternity of the Church."[168]

The position of Athenagoras was different, since he felt challenged by the tragedies of history, particularly of war. He was a child of the multiethnic and multi-religious reality of the Ottoman Empire. As a young deacon he was sent to the Balkans, to Monastir, today, Bitola. He knew the fury of Balkan nationalisms and their repercussions on the Church, especially the fight between the Bulgarian Orthodox Christians and the Phanariots in Macedonia (the Phanariots defined ecclesiastical nationalism as "phyletism"). The nationalization of Macedonia after World War I involved the elimination of every trace of Islam and the Serbification of Orthodoxy. Athenagoras experienced from close up the conflict between the Turks, Serbs, and Bulgarians at the time of World War I (a large cemetery in Bitola contains sixteen thousand French soldiers who died in the war). In this situ-

---

168. Adriano Roccucci, *Stalin e il patriarca. Chiesa ortodossa e il potere sovietico*, 1917–1958 (Turin: Einaudi, 2011), 372.

ation, he developed an awareness of the deep connection between the Church and peace. Throughout his life (he died in 1972) he said, "All people are good." He also argued that all people: ". . . should find their place within human unity. I belong to them all. The drive of human unity must be Christian unity."[169]

The Patriarch was convinced that, "The living heart of human unity must be Christian unity. The unity of humanity is like the expression and the search for our perfect unity in the body of Christ." This was the challenge.

Moreover, after World War II, Athenagoras had the feeling that despite the Cold War, the world was becoming unified ("wars have become the planet's civil wars,") whereas he saw that the Churches remained divided and therefore inert: "We are living in a 'cosmogonic' period: a new world being born before our eyes," he explained to the Catholic cleric Wenger.[170] Clément summed up his thought as follows: There is the advent of planetary man in a globalized history but paradoxically, "every nation clings to its own originality."[171] Nationalisms which, with World War II seemed to have ended, return. Christians should stand at the junction between the globalization movement and their own national identity. Only a spiritual humanism could have smoothed out conflicts, led people and religions to unity, respecting their different identities. In reality, according to the Patriarch, because Christianity was divided, it became absent or not very decisive in the fight against wars and in the fundamental humanization that is peace.[172]

---

169. Olivier Clément, *Dialogues avec le patriarche Athënagoras*, 2nd ed. (Paris: Fayard 1976), 16.
170. Antoine Wenger, *Les trois Rome. L'Eglise des années soixante* (Paris: Desclée de Brouwer, 1991), 59.
171. Ibid., 230.
172. Also see my own: *Il professore e il patriarca*.

The unity of Christians, the unity of humankind and peace: These themes recur again and again in the Christian world of the twentieth century. The limitation of this movement of thought and action is in the difficulty to link the different Christian identities, despite the improvement in their relations. To some extent, what Pope John Paul II accomplished in Assisi in 1986, bringing together the differences of the religions in a global vision of peace, is a point of arrival. It was a unique event in history, as well as the most popular religious symbol of the twentieth century. According to Father Balducci, even though he criticized Wojtyla's pontificate, the Assisi meeting "cannot be compared to anything else," because it expressed a planetary humanism that spoke of peace and coexistence.[173] I do not want to go into this rich and complex period, except to point out that Wojtyla also had a very tough experience during the war in Poland.[174]

In fact, a direct, honest, and personal approach to the drama of war is fundamental. After World War I and II, yesterday and today, true humanism, capable of laying the foundations for peaceful coexistence in the plurality of identities, can emerge. A humanism of peace, that knows how to combine national identities to enable them to live together in a global framework, is needed. It starts with recognizing the humanity of the enemy which, together with one's own and with that of the other, becomes the humanity of the world. This is the ancient Christian secret, kept by Churches albeit divided, which have strained to overcome the divisions, but have not achieved unity.

---

173. Ernesto Balducci, "L'evento di Assisi," in *L'uomo planetario* (S. Domenico di Fiesole: Cultura della Pace, 1994), 166–167.
174. Cfr. Riccardi, *Giovanni Paolo II*.

The great German novelist, Erich Maria Remarque, was a soldier during World War I. and, in *All Quiet on the Western Front*, he portrays a generation marked by that war through the words of a nineteen-year-old soldier who discovers the humanity of the enemy:

> Comrade, I did not want to kill you.... Why didn't they tell us that you are poor souls just like us, that your mothers fear for you like ours for us, and that we have the same terror, and the same death and the same suffering? Forgive me comrade, how could you be my enemy? If we throw down our arms and uniforms, you could be my brother.[175]

---

175. Erich M. Remarque, *All Quiet on the Western Front* (Boston: Litte Brown and Company, 1930), 133.

Nine

A Passionate Seeker of Peace: Giorgio La Pira

The Historiography of the Depths

Much has been published on Giorgio La Pira: documents, memoirs, pleasant recollections, resolutions—from a scholarly to a devotional level. Many conferences have been held. However, there is one question regarding La Pira that we should try to answer if we are to remember him, and want his message to be more than cherished testimonies for a world of devotees and nostalgic people, as often occurs. It is the question about a world, the one after 1989, marked by clashes of civilizations, religions, cultural universes; a world in which the Non-Aligned Movement, set up in Bandung in 1955, no longer exists; in which decolonization seems to have failed some of its objectives; in which identity has a greater value than dialogue; in which Islam no longer has just the tolerant and heroic face of the Sultan of Morocco, Mohammed V, who was once received by the mayor of Florence in his city; in which communism no longer exists.... And so on. In this very different world, does Giorgio La Pira's thought still find a place or should it be relegated to a mere spiritual testimony of other times?

After all, La Pira, with great nobility, can be considered a representative of the times of hopes and dreams that preceded the Second Vatican Council, who also prepared for and experienced the détente after the darkest years of the Cold War. He could be accused of having been not only naïve, which many of his contemporaries reproached him for, but also of a certain optimism with which he looked at history, its protagonists, and the forces involved. That optimism could also be found in the pages of *Gaudium et Spes*, the *Pastoral Constitution on the Church in the Modern World* promulgated in 1965, at the end of the Second Vatican Council. That unification of the world (which the Council partly envisaged and La Pira hoped for) actually turned out to be globalization with strong homologations, marked by many conflicts. On the other hand, La Pira's vision, while open to the Global South, Islam, and Asia, was still marked by a strong Eurocentrism. It is enough to think about his consideration of France's role in the 1950s and 1960s, which for him represented a Catholic country capable of leaving a mark on the history of the world.

These are not ex post facto, out of history questions because everything obviously ages and is outdated with the passing of the years and changing geopolitical situations. One could focus on the testimony of La Pira as a Christian. The fact that a Christian is a man of peace should be all too obvious. La Pira was a man of peace because he was a Christian. The problem is another: Did La Pira, the Christian, a lover of peace, precisely because he was a Christian, understand the deep current of the contemporary world that in some way reached all the way to the present time? In an interview in 1976 with David Sassoli's father, [Mayor] Domenico Sassoli, , the mayor said, "Have you ever thought of the possibility of a historiography of the depths? You know that the movement of the sea follows strict rules. On the surface, the sea looks rough, suggesting chaos, becoming increasingly chaotic at the mercy of uncontrollable forces; but in the depths, there are powerful and mysterious currents that govern the movement of the sea. Equally in the depths of human history, so agitated on the surface, there are strong and mysterious currents that push and pull us in a very precise direction, toward unity and peace. It is necessary to distinguish them"[176]

Was this the metahistorical optimism of a believer who, like in the book of Revelation, trusted in an eschatological ending? This dimension was certainly present in La Pira; indeed it determined his thinking and acting. However, for him culture had a high function—to make a historiography of the depths also in relation to a politician "who stares at the surface and does not see what is happening in the depths."[177] One only needs to think of the relationship between the visionary La Pira and the politician Amintore Fanfani. Did La Pira know how to draw lines of a historiography of the depths?

In his relations with communist Eastern Europe, with the Soviet Union (or Russia, as he insisted on calling it, with the awareness that it had not died in the Soviet Empire) and with Poland, La Pira was not only a dialogist, but someone who had a clear idea about the future of this world. Regarding Poland, he understood how, despite its place in the Soviet imperial system, it could represent the weakest link, precisely because of the strong presence of the Church in its society. So, after the death of Pope Pius XII in November 1958, he wrote to Monsignor Domenico Tardini, to whom Pope John XXIII had entrusted the Secretariat of State: "My love and my prayer—no matter how humble—for Catholic Poland and for its great Cardinal Primate, grow every day. I think that this nation—a true believer in Christ!—is the bridge that our Lord is building in order to allow His Church and His grace a passage

---

176. Giorgio La Pira, *Il Fondamento e il progetto di ogni speranza*, Carlotta Alpigiano Lamioni and Paolo Andreoli, eds. (Rome: Editrice Ave, 1992), 375.
177. Ibid.

toward the immense spaces 'of the Babylonian Empire,' a space in which a billion people live."[178]

In his correspondence, Giorgio La Pira often talks about "nations," a term seldom used by Italians after World War II in a cautious Italy that followed its twenty years of fascism. According to the mayor, nations were still the protagonists of history. In the letter mentioned above, he wrote: "The problem of the Church is also the problem of nations and of civilizations," referring to the three poles of his geopolitical vision: the Church, nations, and civilization. During the conferences in Florence, the role he attributed to nations emerged: That of 1952 was called "the council of Christian nations or those who live in the universal orbit of Christianity." For La Pira, nations are subjects of history, active even if hidden under communist suppression. Regarding the conferences in Florence, one is somewhat surprised by the mayor's difficulty in considering the existence of another religious world in which Christianity means little or is not as fundamental as he says it is. In fact, this sensitivity developed later on, through his travels and contacts with other worlds.

Beyond the Cold War, Conflicts, Clashes of Civilizations

In the eyes of the Soviet world, just as for Italian politicians, La Pira was a convinced anti-communist. He perceived the communist universe as different from the Church and the West, an antagonist to the very core. For him, Khrushchev and Mao Tse-Tung were "bandits." In 1953, at the time of Stalin's death, he wrote to Pope Pius XII: "Communism will no longer win in Italy or abroad. It has reached its 'limit': we

---

178. La Pira to Tardini, November 14, 1958, copy with the author.

are already there...."[179] For La Pira, the struggle had to be carried out not so much in terms of opposition but of "attraction," a key word in the mayor's strategy. In the depths of history—always in his thoughts—there was a unifying movement. It was difficult to avoid, despite political resistance. In his vision, the purpose of the reunification of Europe was to remove the obstacles. In 1966, twenty years before the fall of the Berlin Wall, he wrote to Fanfani: "This road leads to the unity and peacemaking of all Europe (all of it: from the Atlantic to the Urals)...."[180] It is a pan-European vision which, at the time of the Cold War, was shared only by General de Gaulle (La Pira's great interlocutor) and Wojtyla (even though the mayor died shortly before the beginning of Pope John Paul II's pontificate). In this regard, the Second Vatican Council is also considered a great pan-European event, which it was. In 1959, the mayor wrote to Don Loris Capovilla, Pope John XXIII's secretary:

> Thus, the Council is not only interested in the Church. It is an act of extreme interest (if fully understood) for the people and the nations (particularly in Europe—One should not forget that Russia is an essential part of Europe, that its destiny of Christian salvation is linked to Europe—just like Constantinople is linked to Rome!)[181]

---

179. Giorgio La Pira, Andrea Riccardi, and Isabella Piersanti, eds., *Beatissimo Padre: Lettere a Pio XII*, Letter of June 15, 1953 (Milan: Mondadori, 2004), 71 [underlined in the text]. See also my *Introduction* to this book, 15–41.
180. Giorgio La Pira, Amintore Fanfani, Sara Selmi, and Sebastiano Nerozzi, *Caro Giorgio..., Caro Amintore...: 25 anni di storia nel carteggio La Pira-Fanfani*, Letter of April 28, 1966 (Florence: Polistampa, 2003), 301.
181. La Pira to L. Capovilla, October 5, 1959, copy with the author.

For La Pira, it was inconceivable to think of Russia as external to Europe. The Council had its own profound effect on the relationship between people and drew their future geography. La Pira's "historiography of the depths" was full of spiritual tensions. On the other hand, it was not exclusively about spiritual or moral issues but also referred to some long-lasting past movements. One should consider the role of nations despite the ideologies and empires of the Cold War. He was thinking of a role for Poland and its Catholicism to undermine the Soviet system, while perceiving the fragility of Moscow's empire and a coming crisis of communism. One should also add the need, stated many times, for a solution to the conflict between Israelis and Palestinians as the key to peace in the Middle East, and for a new relationship of Europe and the West with the Arab world and Islam.

Peace was to be sought through direct talks between Israelis and Palestinians. La Pira stated this at a time when the hypothesis of such talks had not even been considered. For him, peace in the Holy Land and in Jerusalem would expand throughout the Mediterranean, elevating it to a "space of peace." These are the so-called theses of Florence and the Mediterranean talks that started in 1958. The Florentine thesis dealt with the issue of Palestine, whose solution "can only be political; the possible Arab-Israel political dialogue can only be ... triangular: Israel, Palestine and the other Arab states!"[182] The message was clear. the Arabs could not ignore the existence of Israel, but the Israelis had to talk to the Palestinians and the Arabs.

La Pira was a great friend of Israel and a defender of the security of its state and an admirer of Judaism (if only because

---

182. Cf. "La strada di Isaia," speech given at the Mediterranean colloquium sponsored by IPALMO in January 1973, now in La Pira, *Il Fondamento e il progetto*, 256–271, 262.

he read the holy texts, albeit from a Christian perspective), who founded, among other things, the Jewish-Christian Friendship Association. At the same time this man, whose passport had Israeli and Egyptian visa stamps, which was impossible then but still is today for some Arab countries, understood the strong presence of Islam on the international scene and felt challenged on religious ground by the "mystery" that it represented.

The mayor of Florence, through a collaboration with the French journal "*Etudes Méditerranéennes*," and with the great scholar of Islam Lous Massignon (also through the Florentine expert in Middle Eastern studies Father Giulio Basetti Sani), quickly adopted the vision and analysis of the French Catholics who addressed Islam, which was not well-known in Italy. In short, he was aware of the complexity and roots of the Muslim faith, at a time when it was thought that secularization and the modern world would reduce the role of this religion.

The French had already faced these problems, which, in recent years, were revived with regard to the political prominence of Islam. It was discussed in the debate on the clash of civilizations, which recognized the prominent role of religions in the legitimization of identities.[183] The Social Weeks of the French Catholics, an institution founded in 1904 as an agora of lay Catholics alongside the Church, addressed this issue extensively with a session in Versailles in 1936 dedicated to *Les conflits de civilisation*. In that context the worlds were identified in various civilizations: Muslim (Massignon talked about it), Hindu, Soviet, Buddhist and others. There was the question of where the Catholic Church stood among them. While recognizing that it participated directly in some worlds and some civilizations, the work

---

183. Cf. Huntington, *The Clash of Civilizations*.

of the Social Weeks underlined how Catholicism tended to transcend boundaries and did not make an exclusive block with one or another civilization. These ideas were circulating in France between the two world wars and after World War II.

Some of the people La Pira spoke to among the participants in the Weeks in Versailles were Jacques Maritain, Jean Guitton, and Luis Massignon. The answer that came from Versailles was clear and it was Maritain who gave it lucidly: Catholicism had to be an agent of cooperation among people and civilizations.[184] These texts are very interesting, above all because of the debate that started half a century later, beginning with Samuel Huntingdon's theory of the clash of civilizations.

Moreover, it was a position that had already been adopted by the magisterium itself, even at a time when the Cold War represented a real clash of civilizations, between the Soviet-Eastern one and the West. Pope Pacelli talked about communism as a new Islam conqueror. La Pira had a complex and important relationship with Pope Pius XII during the Cold War, which I tried to illustrate with the publication of the mayor's letters to the Pontiff.[185] In fact, although the mayor's political choices did not coincide with those of the Pope (far more worried about communism), their thinking was still similar. It would not otherwise be possible to explain how Pope Pius XII agreed to receive such copious correspondence from the mayor, indeed making it known, through his collaborators, that he was aware of the content of the letters. In 1946, just after World War II, Pope Pius XII stated the substantial difference between the

---

184. Semaines Sociales de France, *Les conflits de civilisations* (Paris-Lyon: Chronique sociale de France, 1936).
185. Cf. G. La Pira, *Beatissimo Padre*.

Church and the empires. The Pope wondered if an empire, even if established spiritually, "does not leave itself open to a danger of another nature, such as granting exaggerated respect and exclusive attention to everything that belongs to it, and not knowing how to appreciate or even understand what is foreign to it?"[186] In a word, an empire denies otherness; not so the Church.

The Pope said, "If, in certain times and places, one or another civilization, one or another ethnic group or social class has made its influence felt more than others on the Church, that does not mean that it enslaves itself to anyone, neither does it freeze in a moment of history, closing itself to any further development."

He concluded saying, "the general understanding of the Church has nothing to do with the narrowness of a sect, nor with the exclusivity of an imperialism captive to its tradition."[187]

Those were considerations in Pope Pius XII's magisterium related closely to La Pira's opinions. The question of the conflict between different worlds is something Catholicism had reflected on for a long time and it was not limited to the conflict between the East and the West alone. For La Pira, it was clear that new worlds had been emerging since the 1950s: the decolonized countries, the non-aligned countries, China, and others. The Holy See, previously with Pope Pius XII but above all with John XXIII, was careful to recognize the value of these worlds. It renewed episcopates seeking to appoint new bishops in former colonial countries. La Pira,

---

186. DISCORSO DI SUA SANTITÀ PIO XII AI NUOVI CARDINALI, Mercoledì, 20 febbraio 1946, https://www.vatican.va/content/pius-xii/it/speeches/1946/documents/hf_p-xii_spe_19460220_la-elevatezza.html
187. Pio XII, *Discorsi e radiomessaggi di Sua Santità Pio XII* (Città del Vaticano; Tipografia Poliglotta Vaticana, 1964) t. VII, 390–391.

as can be seen from his many speeches and his actions, was aware that apart from the West there are many other worlds, religious and political universes, civilizations, and they also count.

Besides—it may seem obvious today—the mayor insisted on the far-reaching role of religions in historical processes. This intuition could be reduced to a fideistic proclamation about the role of religion. There is no doubt that he was happy to accept this intuition, which does not diminish its value. La Pira was convinced, precisely within the historiography of the depths, of the determining function of religions. This aspect was not of secondary importance in a period in which culture, under the influence of Marxism, but not only, tended to underestimate the historical role of religions. Although, it should be reiterated, La Pira considered the role of economic factors and interventions, some of which he was directly involved in. Nonetheless, he was afraid that the war in Algeria would open a rift between Islam and Europe. Massignon, who knew the Muslim world very well, wrote, "Islam threatens to lead the general rebellion of the exploited against the superior technical oppression…"[188]

Attraction, Dialogue, Building Bridges

According to La Pira, Christianity could play a significant role in the way Europe is being seen by the world and in transcending Western civilization. In 1958, he wrote to Pope Pius XII: "What does the so-called free West have to offer the followers of Islam who gather, praying around their mosques; to the people of Asia who become aware of their 'metaphysical' and contemplative roots; to the communist

---

188. La Pira et al., *Beatissimo Padre*, 39.

space that is animated by a false mystique of social justice and human fraternity?"[189]

Within the framework of the geopolitics of the Cold War, La Pira aimed to create bridges between these worlds by identifying the role of several countries. Thanks to a journey to Morocco, he became convinced that this country could facilitate the relationship between Europe and Islam. He thought Poland could do the same with respect to Eastern Europe. "Bridges" make it easier for the development of the policy of attraction, a key aspect in his vision. He wrote to Pope Pius XII in August 1958 (though the letter was not sent because of the Pope's death):

What must be done to 'defeat' the communist system? It is clear—attract into the orbit of the West (but a West with a Christian, not just a technical and mechanical face!) the orbit of the Asian and African people (not Communists). The more this attraction grows, the more effective it will become, and the better it will pay off. Being spiritually and economically rooted, the two orbits (while remaining distinct) will weaken the communist orbit (Russia, China, satellite countries). This weakening resulting from such attraction will be vastly important. It must be followed with increasing care, regardless of the cost.[190]

This was the great strategy of La Pira toward worlds that were different from the East and the West. There was a strategy toward the communist world. The option of war was impossible because it would have turned into an atomic one. So, in 1961, La Pira wrote to Pope John XXIII: "War cannot and must not be waged: peace must be built; peace is built solidly not by warding off, but by attracting Russia

---

189. Ibid., Letter of April 18, 1958, 252.
190. Ibid., 313.

to Christian Europe and the Christian West."[191] How were we supposed to act with Russia and with China?

In 1958, La Pira wrote to Pope Pius XII:

> How? With bombs? No: by attracting them... How to organize this 'attraction'? I know; the question is dramatic; the problem seems almost insoluble; yet one must come to any, even initial and approximate solution to it. In the meantime, one thing is certain: These communists are divided among themselves.... China is in collision with Russia and fears it; Russia is in collision with China and fears it. Both these states need to integrate economically, culturally, and politically with the other parts of the world.[192]

According to La Pira, Russia had to be weakened in order to bring it closer to Europe: "Russia, then, has the deadly weight of satellite states in permanent revolt. What should be done? Attract these communist states separately. As Yugoslavia was attracted, so gradually attract China and the other satellite countries. Gradually isolate Russia so that Russia will feel its weakness more and more and eventually yield to the liberating attraction of the Christian West."[193]

The great but remote Chinese otherness was very present in La Pira's vision, well before he dealt with Vietnam. In fact, La Pira dramatically sensed the distance between the Church and the People's Republic of China, and he perceived it as a drama considering the potential of Chinese society. China represented the future, according to the mayor, who paid

---

191. Giorgio La Pira, Andrea Riccardi, and Augusto D'Angelo, eds., *Il sogno di un tempo nuovo. Lettere a Giovanni XXIII*, Letter to John XXIII of November 22, 1961 (Cinisello Balsamo: San Paolo, 2009), 295–296.
192. La Pira et al., *Beatissimo Padre*, 314.
193. La Pira et al., *Beatissimo Padre*, 314.

great attention to the developments of this country and the growth of its population. One unknown fact about La Pira is that he worked to make it possible for the Chinese bishops, who no longer had any communication with Rome, to receive an invitation to the Council. As Monsignor Capovilla told me, the replacement, Monsignor Angelo Dell'Acqua, informed him that La Pira had found a way to forward the invitations through the Chinese embassy in Cairo (probably with the help of the Egyptians). The plan was to invite the Chinese bishops nominated before the creation of the so-called People's Church and those ordained in *statu necessistatis*. Cardinal Amleto Cicogani, the secretary of state, partially agreed to try this way.

The Pope did not want to decide personally on La Pira's proposal and submitted it to the congregation for extraordinary ecclesiastical affairs, which rejected it with three votes in favor and nine against (among them Alfredo Ottaviani and Pietro Ciriaci). Dell'Acqua and Capovilla appealed to the Pope who, in the end, gave a negative answer. "I am not infallible. I cannot go against these votes. I am the head of the institution that appointed them. It does not feel right." This is how Capovilla remembers Pope John's refusal.[194] For La Pira, the Council represented an event that would open a dialogue between worlds, beyond the institutional boundaries of the Catholic Church. The presence of the Chinese bishops would be an opportunity to come closer. In any case, the presence of bishops from Poland and from some other Eastern European countries made the Second Vatican Council the first pan-European meeting after World War II.

Dialogue, well before Pope Paul VI's encyclical *Ecclesiam suam*, dedicated to this topic, was considered by La Pira to be the instrument for creating attraction and building bridges.

---

194. Author's interview with Msgr. Loris Capovilla.

With the communist world, the mayor was not thinking of easy softening or a sell-out of the policies that developed during the Cold War. He wrote about Fanfani and Eastern Europe to Pope John XXIII: "He could have established a tough but sincere and constructive dialogue with Khrushchev."[195] It was precisely to Fanfani, in 1957, that he had outlined his idea of dialogue: "This willingness to negotiate, to resolve, to remain realistic is a fundamental fact that must be taken into account as a basic premise of every action."[196]

This was La Pira's realism, not locked up in pessimism. The mayor had a positive opinion of the Khrushchev-Kennedy talk in 1959, and pointed out that it was important not to: "leave the American-Russian political dialogue without a 'metapolitical' basis; that is, without, leaving the underlying issue in the shadows—the 'metaphysical and religious' one."[197] Realism went hand in hand with his religious vision of history.

La Pira was aware that there were several worlds on the international scene, even if public opinion concentrated on the confrontation between the United States and the Soviet Union, and that a policy of wide-ranging dialogue had to be carried out with these worlds. However, as he said in his conversation with Adlai Stevenson, it is first of all necessary to avoid being drawn into a worldwide conflict and end ongoing conflicts, which risk transcending their boundaries: "I stated my point of view extremely frankly: everything that helps peace is valid: everything that helps war is wrong: attract Russia into the Christian Western orbit: attract it two ways, 'technical and mystical': bring peace between Israel and Ishmael: end the Algerian war."[198]

---

195. La Pira et al., *Il sogno di un tempo nuovo*, Letter of May 18, 1959, 133.
196. La Pira et al., *Caro Giorgio... Caro Amintore*, Letter of March 4, 1957, 218.
197. La Pira et al., *Il sogno di un tempo nuovo*, Letter of July 31, 1959, 154.
198. Ibid., Letter of July 30, 1959, 152.

A Christian and a Passionate Seeker of Peace

The conflicts in the Middle East and in Algeria were risky also because of the consequences they could have had in the relationship between different worlds. Above all, according to La Pira, it was necessary to firmly state that the path of war could be taken by the great powers: "Peace can be opposed to no other alternative than peace (the alternative being the destruction of the earth)." At this point, "we must, therefore, negotiate, and negotiate with Russia (an enormous space and nuclear power); we must attract it into the orbit of the West (especially Italy) and make it aware of its Christian roots and its Christian vocation." La Pira contrasts the "proponents of crusades." According to him, "there is no other historical or political solution: And it is because the 'military' solution, which until yesterday conditioned the politics of states, is today (and forever) ruled out."[199]

With realistic reasoning, La Pira, in order to banish war from history, introduces the utopia of peace. However, peace is deeply connected to dialogue between people, worlds, and religions. I repeat, at a time when the religions were largely excluded from weighing in on the balance of power, La Pira had the intellectual courage to consider them a highly important element. So according to him there was no peace without religious freedom. It is interesting to see how, from his first contacts with the Soviets, he presented them with the question of religious freedom, which was denied in communist countries. A letter of 1954 from La Pira to the Soviet ambassador Bogomolov (in Rome from 1954 to 1957 and 1959 to 1963) is revealing:

---

199. Ibid., Letter of November 22, 1961, 296.

The Church anxiously awaits a great act of peace on the part of the governments of democratic countries: the release of the Cardinal Primate of Hungary, the Cardinal Primate of Poland, the Primate of Czechoslovakia, and all the bishops and priests: that they be restored to the free expansion of the apostolate of grace, liturgy, truth and love! Your Excellency, this act—if it comes—I hope it will! —will have immense repercussions on all continents and all people: It will be the true rainbow heralding true peace among nations. For the foundation of peace—its essential premise—it comes from religious peace.[200]

Was such a direct and explicit request appropriate just over a month after Stalin's death? La Pira was like that though: confident, not prejudicially hostile, clear, and direct. There is no peace if there is no religious freedom. One can clearly see how his spiritual fiber, his experience of the world, his realism, made him neither a dreamer nor a petty politician but a man with a vision. So far, I have talked a lot about La Pira's strategy and geopolitical readings, much less about his spirituality. However, I believe his spirituality was an essential component of his stature as a man with a vision. His visions were sometimes very bold, both for the political culture of the time and for ecclesiastical contexts.

Regarding the ecclesiastical world, La Pira's loyalty to the Church should be noted, also after the Council and in the face of conflictual situations in the Florentine Catholic world (like in the case of the *Isolotto*, in which he was not convinced of the solution proposed by Cardinal Emenegildo Florit): He was never a Catholic dissident. This was seen in the referendum on divorce, in which he took a position in line with the Church

---

200. Giovanni Spinoso and Claudio Turrini, *Giorgio La Pira: i capitoli di una vita* (Florence: Firenze University Press, 2022). 904.

directives. There is a very significant testimony of the now forgotten Marcella Glisenti (whose role should be reflected on). It concerns a journey she went on with La Pira to Chile in 1971. Glisenti wrote about La Pira's deep-rootedness in the Church, even in the face of confusing situations.

> More than once it was noted that if Catholics were present in these kinds of battles, they often felt distanced from the Church. However, La Pira taught me to have faith in the Church's deep sensitivity to all the real problems of man. 'We go forward because it is right. Without fear. The Church knows that we are right. The Church agrees. Even if it cannot repeat it to us all the time.' I would also like to testify here how his faith in the maternal and noble quality of the Church . . . has taught many of us not to fall into the sterile polemics of those—though noble and generous but distrustful—who often pointed to Rome's silence as a tragic complicity. . . .. [201]

Giorgio La Pira's deep-rootedness in the Christian faith and in the relevance of the Church was one of the reasons that he was encouraged to find out about other, different, distant worlds, as was his increasing familiarity with realities foreign to Christianity or Europe. Giuseppe Dossetti (who somehow sensed the greatness and the superiority of his former colleague) wrote with great insight: "He felt he had been given the mandate to speak and work for the unity of peoples, for peaceful coexistence between opposing ideologies and systems, to build the unity of the world in cooperation and peace, until all his energy was spent." [202]

---

201. Marcella Glisenti, "Ricordo di un viaggio a Santiago con Giorgio La Pira," *Testimonianze* (1978), nos. 4-5-6-7, 441–451.
202. Giuseppe Dossetti, Preface, in La Pira, *Il fondamento e il progetto*, IX.

It should be emphasized, in conclusion, how La Pira understood important aspects of that "historiography of the depth" which, even during the Cold War, encouraged the emergence of the various religions and civil identities, until then repressed. Alongside the challenge of a nuclear war between the two superpowers, he was aware of all kinds of tensions that could lead to a new war. According to La Pira, negotiation and dialogue, an ancient solution consistently proposed by the twentieth century popes in the face of war, represented the way to keep peace, end war, and also establish new communications between worlds. In short, the political-military aspect of dialogue was only part of the dialogue that had to be religious and cultural as well. This was demonstrated by his conferences in Florence. His spirituality was therefore illustrated by his actions.

La Pira's belief in dialogue between worlds led him to a far-reaching understanding of the concept of "peaceful coexistence," that appeared on the horizon in the rapport between East and West, with particular reference to military and political problems. According to him, "peaceful coexistence" was only part of the coexistence that had to be created between worlds through attraction, bridges, and dialogue. In 1969, he writes:

> It is not just about getting rid of the atomic bombs that exist and no' producing any more: it is about qualitatively changing the structure of 'he world. ... It is not just 'bout not making war. It is about qualitatively transforming the civilization of the world, moving from one civilization built with a view to war to another civilization built with a view to peace.[203]

---

203. Ibid., 132.

This is how La Pira reflected on the art and technique of peaceful coexistence. This for La Pira, was the way to the civilization of peace. He was aware that beyond the West and the communist world, other universes were emerging on the international horizon, claiming their place. Following his actions and proposals, one realizes that Giorgio La Pira set out the prerequisites for a real civilization of coexistence between nations, worlds, and religions. II was his idea of peace in the differences and processes of unification on a worldwide scale.[204] Solid peace is achieved by building a civilization of coexistence and not in the logic of confrontation. La Pira's historiography of the depth understands with foresight, the movements of the contemporary world and proposes a horizon, if not a method, in which to place emerging and conflicting realities, within a civilization of living together. Behind so many speeches, interventions, actions, and journeys, there are not only the fragments of an existence consisting of attempts and failures, but also the occasional success. Above all, there is a robust vision of the future of the world and civilization rooted in his belief, a vision corroborated by his constant engagement with reality and by his investigation of the depth of contemporary history. In order to achieve peace, one must learn to live with the other. This is already a civilization.

---

204. See my own: *Living Together* (London: New City, 2008).

Ten

Community: From Me to Us

From the Dream of Us to the Reality of Me

Talking about community seems crucial nowadays. However, it is a vast and complicated field, a history as long as that of humanity, with roots in distant times that leave marks on the desires and of men and women. Community means necessity, drama, and the passion of many people, and in the most diverse ways. Today, in our Europe, it is a rather contrived idea, even though the dream of overcoming the divisions between European countries, at a historical time, after that of the Common Market and before the European Union, was called precisely the European Economic Community, or European Community.

Community! Which one? Over fifty years have passed since 1968, when I helped establish and then develop the Community of Sant'Egidio. A special story: a community of destiny and solidarity, and above all, of an experience with humanity in various countries throughout world, and in contact with situations of war or of suffering.

The story of Sant'Egidio takes me back to 1968. At that time, community was a very trendy word, dream, and reality. There was a widespread desire for community socialization, especially among young people, at least in Western European countries. The story of 1968 in a category of its own, so much so, that it is repeated in the face of an upheaval—Another 1968? Community, commune, communal life, collectivism, assembly—for a vast number of different motivations and inspirations—were experienced with enthusiasm. The experiences and aspirations that characterized the generation of 1968 were in revolt against the authoritarian models, whether patriarchal or competitive individualism. Above all, they were against traditional institutions: from school to university, the family, the armed forces, the police, the Church, and so on. It was a revolt against what was seen as bourgeois, familial, career individualism, in the dream of creating a new "us,": a different "us" from the one inherited from the tradition and society of Western Europe as it had reestablished itself after World War II.

Almost a tabula rasa of the past, a new start—times long gone. Since 1968, several conflicting movements have emerged. On the one hand, community socialization expressed by the desire to live together, as seen in the emergence of collective experiences or organizations; on the other hand, a strong individualism, a different individualism, as in a slogan on a wall of the Sorbonne: "We will have a good master, when each is his own."[205] For many people, and I agree, part of the individualism of our days contradictorily has its roots in 1968.

The life-force of 1968 did not feel the need to explain itself against the categories of the past, or of the culture, which it rejected. The writing on the wall of a secondary school in Paris read, "I have something to say but I don't know what." All this caused bewilderment in a generation of cultured people, who were open-minded but not prepared to forsake debate. A French professor, Olivier Clément, told me about the drama of discussions with his students in 1968, where he would be interrupted by them in a prejudicial way because he was a teacher and represented the system.

In 1968, with the desire to grasp the future, the best-known slogan was: "Be realistic, demand the impossible."

---

205. Julien Besançon, *Les Murs ont la parole, journal mural. Mai 68. Sorbonne, Odéon, Nanterre, etc.* (Paris: Tchou, 1968).

Mario Perniola, a philosopher of my generation, attributed much of populism and irrationalism to the legacy of 1968.[206] This is not the place to discuss this, although I am interested in reminding that the climate of those years was the "us," the collectives, the communal life. It was almost as though the institutions, with their bureaucracy or their politics, had deprived the community of the interpersonal dimension of "us." In the Catholicism after the Council, so chaotic and vibrant, alternatives to institutions were developing. A world of grassroots communities, thriving in the 1960s, spread throughout Latin America and in general in the Global South, as if creating another Church, one with a communitarian face.[207]

Talking about community, living together, collectivism was then normal for the emerging generations. Today we realize how far we are from that world. We are in a season that is going in a different direction from communal socialization. Vincenzo Paglia, a number of years ago, in a book with a very telling title, *Il crollo del noi*, talked about the collapse of "us".[208] The widespread desire for community or communal socialization no longer exists because we live in a distinct season of individualism, not only in Europe but, with due differences, practically throughout the world, so much so that individualism is emerging even in strong family and clan-based societies such as those in Africa. The connection between the affirmation of man as consumer on the one hand and the market on the other hand is obvious. In half a century, there has been a reversal from the community to the individual.

---

206. Mario Perniola, *Berlusconi o il '68 realizzato* (Milan: Mimesis, 2011).
207. Agostino Giovagnoli, *1968 fra utopia e Vangelo. Contestazione e mondo cattolico* (Rome: AVE, 2000).
208. Vincenzo Paglia, *Il crollo del noi* (Bari: Laterza, 2017).

This may be too schematic because different drives coexist within every period, every person, and every culture. Nonetheless, we need to look at the situation from a more general perspective. Luigi Zoya, a psychoanalyst I greatly esteem, developed a significant analysis in a small book called *La morte del prossimo* (Death of the neighbor).[209] Zoja says that, in numerical terms, the "neighbor" has grown; meanwhile, stable relationships have become weaker. The death of the "neighbor" is also the end of community boundaries, which naturally always change, and which have accompanied our existence like a backdrop and created a network.

Above all in the last decades, another phenomenon has occurred—the increase in the "neighbor" in a boundless world that has become a global village.[210] The experience of intense and virtual communications has brought people into contact with images of countries far away, even tragic images, of misery and violence, in front of which one finds it difficult to react because one does not believe it is possible to do anything. In the global era, humanitarian dramas and wars no longer generate intense reactions, despite the fact that they are very close by, since one knows a lot about them. In short, my "neighbor" is also delocalized, so they may be far away. The connections are not those of belonging to a community, but simple bonds of humanity.

Who Is My Neighbor?

"Who is my neighbor?" the scribe asks Jesus in the Gospel according to Luke, when he wants to put Jesus to the test and disprove the obligation of love that the Rabbi had referred to. A decisive question for the Gospel, so much so that the

---

209. Luigi Zoja, *La morte del prossimo* (Turin: Einaudi, 2009).
210. McLuhan and Fiore, *War and Peace*.

Rabbi narrates, in the form of a parable, the story of the Good Samaritan who was the only one to stop beside a dying man on the roadside, unlike the priest and the Levite. At the end of the parable Jesus asks, "Who was the neighbor for that man dying on the road between Jericho and Jerusalem?"

Who is my neighbor in this immense world? A world with no neighbors nearby or with too many neighbors far away. Zoja is right; the family, community, and environmental ties are becoming weaker. The various ways of being a neighbor are becoming weaker. Of course, there is also an aspect of exhilarating freedom. However, in Europe the problem for most people is not emancipation (although it is never completely resolved). "In a society where ties are experienced as constraints or as contracts, being autonomous is perceived as a highly desirable social quality."[211] In the patriarchal African world that encompasses people, family links are still strong. In Europe today, we are freer but more alone. Moreover, it is the exaltation of competition, encouraged by our education, in particular of young people, for whom too many ties can hinder individual affirmation. However, there is a human price to pay for competition without a safety net, about which little is said.

Instead, I would like to mention the crisis of community connections, the death of the neighbor, as a deep and painful limit of society. We talk about the radicalization of young Islamists in European societies, children of immigrants. Radicalization happens in the outskirts of the cities, through personal contact with the Islamic network and internet. Therefore, we must look at the outskirts of the cities, which are a large part of our world today. In 2006, for

---

211. Miguel Benasayag and Gérard Schmit, *L'epoca delle passioni tristi* (Milan: Feltrinelli, 2004), 101.

the first time in history, the population of cities exceeded that of the countryside.

We are an urban world as never before. An urban world is often a universe of outskirts. The slums, consisting of makeshift homes where urbanized people live crowded together, people who have no personal connection, are where 31.6 percent of the world population live. Africa is where this phenomenon is most extreme. Most African men and women live in the outskirts of cities and 71.9 percent of the population of sub-Sahara live in slums. The outskirts generally mean an absence of community ties. It happens easily in Africa, where urbanization puts an end to rural, traditional and community ties.

Let's talk about the European outskirts. I found out about the outskirts of Rome, as described by Pasolini, at the end of the 1960s. A harsh world, with its poor neighborhoods, was not without its networks, communities, and connections. Those were vast networks, created by political or religious volunteers as well as the post 1968 groups. The political parties, above all the Communist Party, organized life with a widespread model second only to the parish, whereas the mayors and committees set up important links and created solidarity. It was a poor world but not of absolute loneliness. All this ended over twenty years ago.

Today the outskirts are experiencing the impact of immigrants. Integration is carried out by the schools and by the community, less by the institutions or by anonymous organizations. In Italy, the integration process has partly succeeded because of the high number of immigrants (above all women) working as caregivers and home helpers; therefore, integration has taken place thanks to families and their network of relationships. It is precisely with new social groups, like immigrants, that we see the poverty of the human fabric of the outskirts, where integration is only partial or does not take place at all. It is worth pointing out that where there is a social void, the mafia networks move in.

Even in the *banlieues* of Paris, where many people are radicalized (if one excludes ethnic groupings), they are nowadays a desert as far as community ties are concerned. Until a few decades ago though, they were inhabited by the vast political network of unions and parties, of associations and religious communities. There were problems then as well; but there were movements that somehow represented a common destiny and offered spaces for solidarity. The traditional and rural networks dissolved with urbanization, and the ones that were a result of political, social, and religious volunteer work, mostly faded away. Apart from school and fragile families, the problem for young people is the lack of communities that are not virtual or function as separate ghettos. Every neighborhood in the outskirts has its own character and history, but the main condition is generally one of loneliness and the absence of social networks.

Another social reality of our times is the situation of the elderly. Longer life-expectancy is fulfilling mankind's old dream and is the result of improved in living conditions. The other side of the coin, however, is that the elderly are often the lonely because as the years go by, the social and family fabric thins out. To continue living in one's own home, one has a vital need for neighbors. It is difficult, almost impossible, to live alone when you are old: As a proverb says, "even the queen needs a neighbor."

The living conditions for the elderly, in my opinion, are a revealing element of the quality of a society or of a civilization. It shows a contradictory process: The achievement of longevity is a dream come true but also a great fragility. I am thinking for example of the question of pensions, which in many African countries exist only for state employees. The elderly who are unable to provide for themselves become a burden and sometimes are removed (if not physically, then accused of witchcraft). As I have already said, it is impossible to live alone, especially when you are old. The elderly show a deep need for the community or a social network. Also, the poor are often lonely people. Poverty and solitude go together. While loneliness generally makes people poor, those who are not poor become so.

I have talked about a shift toward a society of the individual. These and other deep changes have not occurred by chance. Between the end of the last century and this one, there has been a profound revolution, a silent and overpowering affirmation of the global world. We have often failed to notice it and have ignored the human and anthropological repercussions of this process as the relations between everything have changed. The walls of the environment in which we live have fallen, and we have been exposed to winds coming from far away. Previously we felt protected by the existence of a perimeter, as in a horizon or a community. The affirmation of the global world and the new individualism is the reality that Zygmunt Bauman described in *In Search of Politics*.[212] Alain Touraine, in *La globalizzazione e la fine del sociale* (Globalization and the end of society)[213] indicated the implications of the global process, whose impact has not been investigated much at the existential level.

Touraine wrote: "Family, friends, school, or the professional environment everywhere seem to be in a crisis, leaving the individual, young or old, without a spouse or family, whether a foreigner or an immigrant, in a loneliness that leads to depression or the pursuit of artificial or dangerous

---

212. Zygmunt Bauman, *In Search of Politics* (New York: Polity Press, 1999).
213. Alain Touraine, *La globalizzazione e la fine del sociale. Per comprendere il mondo contemporaneo*, trans. Tina D'Agostini and Monica Fiorini (Milan: Il Saggiatore, 2004).

relationships...."[214] Touraine understood very early the consequences of globalization on the community, emphasizing the process of individualization of the citizen-consumer, increasingly so in a digital network but without a social and human one....

The Great Change and Subsequent Reactions

The problem, while the networks were dissolving, was that we were unable to prepare for the great anthropological and economic revolution induced by globalization. It seemed for many people to be a naturally positive evolution with which there was no need to negotiate—almost providential. In any case, how is it possible to negotiate when one is alone and when loneliness was not felt as a limitation? The great social movements, including protest movements, have partially dissolved, and we find ourselves more alone, facing the global revolution.

The history of the second half of the twentieth century was also one of great peace movements that sometimes were able to influence political decisions. The protests against the war in Vietnam is one example. The United States war on Iraq in 2003 led to protests on the streets involving thirty million people in eight hundred cities throughout the world. Fifteen years later, confronted by the war in Syria (ongoing since 2011), we must acknowledge the inertia of the collective movements in the face of the horror of a country devastated by a senseless war. It can be argued that the Syrian political situation is complex, and it was not easy to take sides. Nonetheless this reveals a widespread inability to make people, communities, or movements, move together toward an

---

214. Ibid., 93.

aim. The war in Syria shows the weakness of public opinion and that of an international community which, in so many ways, seems to have regressed. Some consequences of that war, I am thinking of the Syrian refugees, have also affected Europe (but it has reacted with blockades and walls instead of addressing the central issue, which is the destruction of an entire country).

Perhaps, with the advent of globalization, many networks dissolved because they could not cope with it or because they were obsolete, compared to the imposition of new horizons that were initially looked at optimistically. The world was supposed to become all democracy and markets, banishing the fears of the Cold War and the borders inherited from history. Then, let us not forget, for those who were not born in the digital age, the rise of social media that offered the possibility of making new connections, without direct, physical involvement.

Actually, we were often unconsciously subject to the global revolution. We experienced it without understanding it as a connected process, merely noticing some effects here and there when our existence ran up against it. The optimism of globalization, for a few years the result of generally widespread laziness, has given way to many fears that have been accompanying men and women all over the world for some time now. Fear of the great story of the globalized world, led by invisible hands, a tsunami able to overwhelm our little, unprotected universes. In fact, security becomes a priority in any political proposal which can be sold to the voters, even though our European cities are mostly safe. When people talk about insecurity with regard to Italian cities, they show they do not know about life in the cities of the Southern Hemisphere.

In the end, the public security answer does not calm people's deep-seated fear, fear measured by phenomena that seem to be too big—first and foremost, migrations portrayed as real invasions. There is a dissatisfaction with the complex processes of democracy, deemed too slow and ineffective, while there is a move toward decision-making by strong personalities and policies.

Fear is nothing new, as from the beginning to the end of the Bible, one of the most recurrent invitations is to not be afraid. Politics equips itself to give answers to society, identifying threats and affirming the need, in the global world, to regain control of one's space within which to protect oneself. The threats being foreigners, immigrants, and Romani people. (Whether the latter represent a danger is to be proven: In my opinion it is only an indication of the incapacity to manage a social policy for a few thousand, especially young people). The political narrative insists on protecting the national space. It is the story of Eastern European countries, starting with Hungary, which has built a wall to defend itself from immigrants. Especially in Eastern Europe, the narrative of European, white, and Christian identities threatened by invasions of foreigners and Muslims is very common.

The revival of the racial category of whiteness, which sounds absurd to us (it is worth pointing out that Italy, after the United States, was the second country in the world for international adoptions) is not uncommon, as the history of a few European countries proves: Starting with Italy, which in 1938 applied racist laws against Jews following the Manifesto of Race, which postulated the existence of an Aryan race of Nordic origin to which Italians belonged. The fascist regime introduced harsh legislations against mixed marriages between Italians and Ethiopians and Eritreans, claiming there was a risk of contamination. I cannot fail to recall how, in 1937, in response to an attack, Italian colonial troops slaughtered Africans in Addis Ababa and massacred two thousand people in the nearby monastery, Debre Libanos, under the banner of contempt for "nonhumans."[215]

Significantly, I say this in passing but it is an important fact, the Minister of Defense, Lorenzo Guerini, acknowledged Italian and Fascist responsibilities in those sad events. For his part, Cardinal Bassetti, on behalf of the Italian bishops, declared how the Italian Church was insensitive to the drama of aggression and repression by the fascists of a free country like Ethiopia.

During World War II, Italy was partly liberated by African troops in the service of France, perhaps relatives of the Senegalese immigrants who are among us today. In Germany, after World War I, people were ashamed of having been defeated by French soldiers of African descent, and very harsh measures were applied to the few Africans living in the country, such as castration and internment. Few people know that there were Africans in the Nazi concentration camps.[216]

Responding to the fears of man means proposing an identity that often qualifies as "against," putting together heterogeneous elements. It is not a question of building or rebuilding a community but the feeling of being part of a tribe that has been lost and whose existence is postulated as having always existed. So many people, fearing/hating some threatening individuals, look to a leader and feel reassured to be part of a tribe/nation—perhaps against others. The world of European individuals—with the new politics of strong men or populisms—is divided into tribes that have enemies to fight or to defend themselves from, but it often does not mean existential experiences of new and reassuring bonds. The new tribes are the reality of lonely individuals.

---

215. Paolo Borruso, *Debre Libanos 1937: Il più grave crimine di guerra dell'Italia* (Rome-Bari: Laterza, 2020), IX
216. Serge Bilé, *Neri nei campi nazisti* (Bologna: EMI, 2006).

Maurizio Molinari talked about *Il ritorno delle tribu.* (The return to the tribes.)[217] The tribe reassures, and it responds to the emptiness of life without relationships. Often however, it is a case of vertical identification that does not correspond to a human, associative, community network. It is politics, divorced from culture, and reduced to a football match, said Giuseppe De Rita and Antonio Galdo, consisting of insults, hateful talk, rude language, friends, and enemies.[218] Between the return of tribes and neo-individualism, one wonders if the very idea of community is not something remote, belonging to other ages, the result of nostalgia or a utopia.

A Community Revolution?

Martin Buber, a Jewish thinker with roots in Eastern European, German, and Israeli worlds, who identified intersubjectivity as the scenario of existence, left us with the image of the Hasidim world (the devout, mystical Jews of Eastern Europe), destroyed in the Holocaust. His literary world, which is a reinterpretation, offers a picture of these particular communities, which as a young man, he had observed closely: "Never in Europe has a broad community of people—not an order of hermits, not a confraternity of the chosen, but a community of people in all its spiritual and social multiplicity, in all its variegated composition—founded the whole of life as a unity, on what one has inwardly come to know."[219]

---

217. Maurizio Molinari, *Il ritorno delle tribù: La sfida dei nuovi clan all'ordine mondiale* (Milan: Rizzoli, 2017).
218. Giuseppe De Rita and Antonio Galdo, *Prigionieri del presente: Come uscire dalla trappola della modernità* (Turin: Einaudi, 2018).
219. Martin Buber, *Hasidism and Modern Man*, ed. Maurice Friedman (Princeton: Princeton University Press, 2015), 18.

This is the image that struck the young Buber—a reality destroyed by the Nazi massacres during World War II. Throughout his life however, Buber wondered about the question of community, also looking at the kibbutz, before and after the proclamation of the State of Israel. The kibbutz seemed to him to be a response to individualism and collectivism but also to the overwhelming power of planetary forces and the illusory myth of endless progress. It is not a model to be applied generally but a community dimension to be understood and cultivated. Buber concluded, "Our community does not want a revolution but is a revolution."[220] In other words, community tension, whatever it is, is a movement that changes reality.

In 1930, facing the rise of totalitarianisms, Buber wrote, "The world itself has the nostalgic desire to become a community."[221] But what does community mean? Some historical, religious or collectivist model? Referring to these models, Buber pursues the idea that community tension in life is essential for the person and vital for society. When he was young, he wrote, "Here is the community; here is what we want."[222] Mature, free men who go with the flow of giving and receiving in a logic of reciprocity. Over the years, the community dimension of existence as a reality and utopia emerges strongly, whereby the waiting for the Messiah also becomes waiting for the community. Buber's communitarian messianism is condensed into this expression: "Do what is possible and desire what is impossible."[223]

Does the communitarian ideal become an anti-globalization dream today, a nostalgia that almost demands

---

220. Quoted in Martin Buber, *Sentieri in utopia. sulla comunità*, ed. Donatella Di Cesare (Genova: Marietti, 2009), 18.
221. Martin Buber, *Communauté* (Paris: Eclat, 2018), 59.
222. Ibid., 22.
223. Buber, *Sentieri in utopia*, 15.

leaving the world? This is what in the United States, some traditional Christians, mainly Catholics preach, namely the Benedict Option, which was the choice of St. Benedict who founded a community of monks outside the city of Rome.[224] Often, throughout history, frightened by what seems to be the prevailing chaos, or caught up in the attraction of a dream, men and women have sought to establish "fortified communities." Lost paradises, fortresses, hells? The community cannot be an escape from the world, an idea which, in fact, has always been limited to a handful of dreamers. From the fourth century onward, in the Christian world, it was the monks who practiced the *fuga mundi* [flight from the world] from a Christianity that they considered corrupted by city life and customs.

There is a yearning for community around us and in us, wrote Bauman and he is right. It is something deep, that comes from far away, as we read in Genesis. When God saw the man he had created, he said, "And the LORD God said, "It is not good that man should be alone; I will make a helper suitable for him" (Genesis 2:18). Man had found no help to match him in the wild animals, beasts, or birds of the air. Therefore, God created woman. Tzvetan Todorov, a French-Bulgarian intellectual showed how man lives by being together with others and needs their consideration.[225]

There is the need to inhabit the global world in a less anonymous, less isolated way. There is a community dimension to cultivate and grow, which cannot be just a legacy of the past to be preserved but must be something to be reinvented. The communitarian dimension is a dream, a tension

---

224. Rod Dreher, *The Benedict Option: A Strategy for Christians in a Post-Christian Nation* (New York: Sentinel, 2017).
225. Tzvetan Todorov, *Noi e l'altro. Scritti e interviste* (Rome: Datanews, 2007).

or aspiration, a bond, a fabric of reciprocity, a model. Paglia said, "Globalization has brought us closer together as one *us*: one humanity. Yet it seems that the us is depleted of its strength. Indeed, that it has collapsed."[226]

Emmanuel Mounier, in the twentieth century, talked about a necessary personalistic and communitarian revolution. Today, inhabiting the global world involves developing the communitarian dimension within the framework of our relationships and existence. As I mentioned, in order to inhabit such a world, there is a widespread need to rebuild the community, although establishing the community or living its tension requires a great capacity to integrate with the other.

Only through the communal dimension can we understand such an experience of common humanity without borders and better understand what unites us with our distant neighbor. Experiences of openness to global humanity need, on the other hand, realizations, or tensions of a communitarian us. Communal proximity makes one open, not closed, in the face of the global world; on the contrary, it is the premise of widening horizons.

De Rita and Galdo conclude their analysis of a world of egos, prisoners of the present, with a proposal that may seem simple, almost elementary: to begin again from the "me," from the conscious subject, even from individualism, not to limit the horizon of individuals to well-being or self-sufficiency, but to reconstruct an "us." Sisyphus' fatigue in such a complex world? The authors continue, "Life is always changed within the framework of social processes, and not through external shortcuts."[227]

---

226. Paglia, *Il crollo del noi*, 22.
227. Giuseppe De Rita and Antonio Galdo, *Prigionieri del presente* (Turin: Einaudi, 2018) 86.

Community: From Me to Us

In terms that may perhaps appear simplistic, Bauman, in his essay called *Retrotopia*, proposed the resumption of cultivating a dialogical and communal dimension in everyday life.[228] He did so in his discussion with Pope Francis, in which the latter affirms the centrality of a culture of dialogue and encounter: "This culture is possible if we all participate in its elaboration and construction." Bauman wrote:

> The underlying intention of Pope Francis's message is to transfer the fate of coexistence, solidarity, and peaceful cooperation among men from the vague and obscure realm of big politics, the politics you see on television, to the streets, workshops, schools, and public spaces where we hoi polloi meet and talk: to take the issue, the fates and hopes of humanity's integration, out of the hands of those who command the troops of the Clash of civilizations . . . to entrust them to the everyday encounters between neighbors and colleagues . . . as attentive or insensitive parents, loyal or disloyal companions, caring or petty neighbors, disagreeable or boring colleagues, and certainly not to representatives of civilizations, traditions, faiths or ethnicities that are separated by mutual estrangement.[229]

This is what it means to inhabit the global world: not herded into tribes, but to be within a community dimension in which the "me," the subject, the individual, takes back the initiative, not as a consumer of life but as a builder, moving in a tension toward the "us" through the experience of encounter. Among the many observers of our time who converge on the need to start again from the "me,"—my own

---

228. Zygmunt Bauman, *Retrotopia* (Cambridge: Polity Press, 2017).
229. Ibid., 167–168.

self and that of others—I want to mention Pankaj Mishra, who states that it takes a manner of thinking that is capable of transforming the "me" and the "us."[230] To begin again from the "me" is a decision that no one can deny, but it complements other decisions and can take one far.

---

230. Mishra, *Age of Anger*

Eleven

Visions Beyond the Wall of the Impossible

Humanity Suffers Mostly from a Lack of Vision

There is a widespread need for vision in society. There are of all kinds of visions, and a historian of religious phenomena like me knows this quite well: secular, religious, political, corporate……However, the problem today is the lack of vision. We are prisoners of the present, a dense present surrounded by walls that tell us the future is not possible or is too dangerous. Ours is the horizon of the eternal present. At the end of their book *Prigionieri del presente* (Prisoners of the present),[231] Giuseppe De Rita and Antonio Galdo write, "Too little and too short to be able to grow again."

I am reminded of a quote by Karol Wojtyla,, a man not well-recognized as a poet; and yet, in the heavy years of his life in Poland under the communist regime, he wrote, "I believe that man suffers above all from a lack of vision." This was the 1960s, and there were no prospects for change on the horizon; the country's history seemed to be crystallized; Soviet control over society and politics was powerful. For Wojtyla, and many like him, the horizon was bleak, without visions of hope, which led him to say—it may seem an exaggeration—that man suffers above all because a vision is lacking. He suggested, however, that one can accept a difficult period if searches for visions, which are

---

231. De Rita and Galdo, *Prigionieri del presente*.

the beacon of hope, plans for the future, or at other times, lights at the end of a tunnel.

In recent years we have also been suffering from lack of vision, although in a different way. Today history has changed a lot compared to the years Wojtyla wrote those words. We historians still talk about contemporary history, but today one could say that it has become post-contemporary: actually, global after 1989. It is a dimension that still needs to be explored properly, also with regard to the human condition of the global man and woman. However, so much has changed in life.

The horizon of Poland in the 1960s was very limited; only selected information filtered through. It was different in the West but, even in this case, the horizon was not limitless as it is today. The facts and news were mainly national. Our country lay comfortably within its borders, separate from Eastern Europe, within the scenario of the Europe of the Six. It was another world before globalization. In today's global world however, there is a sense of being able to see everything, whatever the distance between us. Far away facts and events reach us, and the news multiplies. Whatever is happening in the distance intrudes on our horizon. The person who represents the distance coming toward us, is increasingly the immigrant. So much available news does not mean that it is easy for us to process a thought or a vision. I mean, we see without a vision.

It is possible to see a lot and very far, but how can we filter the excess information? How can we organize it? Sometimes people talk about information overload. I am not an expert on these topics, but it is also my experience. So, from an international point of view, we are shocked to see horrendous tragedies that we know a lot about. We can see the images of them almost from close up and hear their voices. What can we do? I will not dwell on the dramatic story of the war in Syria, which has been underway since 2011. It is not an isolated case. I would like to mention at least two other wars, both taking place in the global age. First of all, the genocide in Ruanda, one hundred terrible days with five hundred thousand deaths in 1994. How can one understand an ethnic war between Hutus and Tutsis? Even in those days, we found ourselves looking at terrible images. Then the war in former Yugoslavia—and again the public was very confused.

On the other hand, a distant war, like Vietnam in the 1970s, was much clearer. Those who were with the West were with South Vietnam, the others were with North Vietnam. An ideological vision filtered the images and information. Ideology was a great instrument for elaborating and sorting information.

The time for visions made up in the workshops of ideology, conveyed and manipulated by politics, is over for good. No nostalgia. We have lived through years not only of broadening horizons but also of demystification. Today, however, faced with so much information, we perceive we are trapped within the wall of the impossible, the one of our present here and now. I see people becoming disoriented. The French-Bulgarian writer Tzevan Todorov talked about "*L'uomo spaesato*" ("disoriented man").[232] Not lost in the darkness of a world that he cannot see, but on the contrary in the light, in too much light. There is so much information; so many lights are turned on by the media. An English art critic John Ruskin wrote, "It is the excess of light that makes life today perfectly vulgar."

The present is often drained and blinded by an excess of light, like fireworks. In short, a lot of light but very few

---

232. TzvetanTodorov, *L'uomo spaesato: i percorsi dell'appartenenza* (Rome: Donzelli, 1997).

visions. Seeing a lot of things even at a great distance does not mean nurturing visions. From a point of view of communication, one is often besieged by seeing and hearing. This unexpressed suffering of men and women of our times can be found, in different terms, in the debate between the political forces that come together and fall apart. The lack of vision often means an absence of a healthy relationship between politics and culture. The relationship between politics and ideology has disappeared in favor of one between politics, the media, and social media. What emerges is an aggressive climate, as that of football fans, rather than that characterized by the battles of ideas or of projects for the future. However, the problem is not just about politics. It is a question that involves everyone. It is difficult to make a vision mature.

With No Visions but with Limitless Horizons

Is the situation not a result of the complex times we live in? Yesterday our horizons were restricted to our country, region, or town. How can we have a vision today when our horizons are limitless and globalized? Is the search for a vision not part of a culture and policy connected to nineteenth century models? Are we not reasoning with old categories? Is there no hidden nostalgia for ideological visions? Therefore, one wonders whether we prefer myths to visions.

I wonder whether nowadays we are not looking for answers to the needs born in the past, which we still carry within us. In this sense I think—and I have already said so—our generation, born and raised before the global world, having lived through these two such particular decades, is a bit of an "exodus generation." It is a generation that experienced a different time from today, the time before globalization, which has revolutionized spaces, possibilities, perspectives. It is worth returning for a moment to Wojtyla, the poet, who continued his thoughts as follows: "

> If he suffers from the lack of vision / he then
> must pave his way among the signs
> Until what gravitates inside, matures as fruit
> of the word.
> This is the weight that Jacob felt when the stars,
> weary like the eyes of his flock, fell onto him."[233]

The condition Wojtyla decries—like that of many intellectuals, whether believers or not, thinkers of Eastern Europe during the 1960s—was that of an extreme poverty, of visions but also of a silence of words and of debates. I met Bronislaw Geremek, a Polish historian of Jewish origin, around ten years younger than Wojtyla, whose religious vision he did not share, but whose decisive role he recognized. I saw in him thoughtful research, developed during the years in which he was freeing himself, opposing a communist ideological vision and looking for another vision of the future, while cultivating his historical studies. And he found it, first in his historical research and then in the political struggle of the 1980s and in the Solidarity Movement.

Whoever loves history is convinced that it has something to say to the present and helps us look toward the future. Umberto Eco said one must not underestimate the old saying, *Historia magistra vitae*, [history is the teacher of life]. However, it is not to be understood in a flat and scholastic sense, as though it were a lesson for the future, but in the sense that historical visions show how time is always complex—the past, as well as the present and the future.

---

233. Karol Wojtyła, *Tutte le opere letterarie. Poesie, drammi e scritti sul teatro* (Milan: Bompiani, 2001), 117.

Historical memory, with its complexity, certainly protects us from simplifications—sometimes terrible ones like the friend-foe one—smuggled in by the simplifiers of our time. Emotional representations of reality.

Europe today is not marked by the silence or absence of debates or information, as was the communist Eastern Europe of Geremek or Wojtyla. Nonetheless, one can see—in my opinion—a deep suffering caused by the lack of vision, not only in Italy but in Europe as a whole. In its long history, Europe has woven within its visions of the future an outreach to civilization beyond its borders, including the areas of economics, science, culture, politics, and colonial. European immigration was also the result of a vision of the future, which in some way coincided with that of a particular country (let us say, promised), as America or other parts of the world. It makes one wonder today about the vision of immigrants who come from the Global South. I am thinking for example about how Africans might look at Europe, which they are prepared to reach going on long journeys across the desert and the sea—visions of Europe. What impact does reality have on these visions? I have read with passion and pain the stories of immigrants detained for months in inhumane conditions in Libya. I saw their naïve dreams fall apart in a universe that is no different from a concentration camp.

Paolo Prodi, a historian who studied the modern and contemporary history of Europe, concentrated in one of his last speeches on the end of the propulsive visions of our world today. In his essay *Il tramonto della rivoluzione* ("The decline of the revolution") he wrote that nothing is stable in modern European history.[234] On the contrary, instability has been the driving force of the growth of Europe. The

---

234. Paolo Prodi, *Il tramonto della rivoluzione* (Bologna: Il Mulino, 2015).

Judeo-Christian idea of history as a path to salvation has so often broken the cyclical sense of time, introducing elements and impulses for progress, for breaking with the heavy present and offering paths forward.

It is the great theme of the prophecy that rises from the Bible and communicates itself in the Christian world and beyond. The prophet speaks through visions that illuminate the present and offer glimpses of the future. The *Book of Sirach* in the Bible calls the prophet Isaiah (there are many prophetic authors with his name), "great and faithful in his vision" (48:22). Certainly, in the history of biblical Israel there were also periods when there was a lack of prophets and visions. The Christian Bible concludes with *Revelation*. It is a book of visions that allows us to see the light of the future in a dark and gloomy present. Today the word "Apocalypse" ("*Apocalisse*" in Italian—in English "Revelation") has come to mean an immeasurably serious event.

Prophecies and prophetism have become deeply embedded in European society starting from the reference to the God of the Bible. They have come a long way, leaving the area of religious tradition, without losing their mobilizing drive. The prophetic tension, over the centuries and in various histories, has been secularized into utopias. It is no longer only a question of redemption at the end of the world but also the coming of a better era, consisting of well-being, justice, a new humanity, progress, and freedom. In short, an alternative society. This is where the deep relationship between vision and utopia lies. . . . The secularization of prophetic tension in revolutionary utopias moves messianism toward politics.

The intertwining of prophecies and utopia animates the tension typical of modern European history.

Regaining History Opens Us to the Vision of the Future

Paolo Prodi, starting from the *Remarques sur l'histoire* ("Comments on history") (1749), in which Voltaire wrote about the world saying, "everything concerns us and is done for us," affirmed that today we need to rediscover "the soul of Europe as it emerges from Voltaire's pages." There is something very deep and vital in his words, covering all fields of European life over the last centuries. Prodi aimed to reintroduce a thread of European history either to pick it up again or to definitively consider it interrupted. He said: "[Voltaire] calls this soul of Europe a 'permanent revolution'. At the center of this long-term European history, there is the process of the development of the political pact, but the roots of this process lie in this revolutionary tension."[235]

Revolutionary tension (not just political revolutions, but the drive toward change), prophecies, utopia, and visions are inextricably intertwined. Talking about it might seem nostalgic in today's Europe that is allergic to tension, worried about being challenged by the great history around us, often driven to close in on itself. Today—according to Prodi, whatever one calls it—we are faced with the end of this tension which produces visions of the future. He himself, together with Massimo Cacciari, concludes in this manner a book called *Occidente senza utopie* (The West without utopias).[236]

I am well aware that the West for a century has been complaining about the end of visions, utopias, and dreams. However, complaining is also a way of invoking or preparing for a vision. Over one hundred years ago, Oswald Spengler

---
235. Ibid., 54–55.
236. Massimo Cacciari and Paolo Prodi, *Occidente senza utopie* (Bologna: Il Mulino, 2016).

published the first volume of *Il tramonto dell'Occidente* (The decline of the West). In the aftermath of Germany's defeat in World War I, and after the European spiritual crisis in 1918, Spengler saw the end of a cycle. Yet, in the very drama of World War I, Europe had a vision of the future—a unified destiny of its economies and democracies, culminating in the European Union, which was also a vision of Europe's place in the world.

What is people's shared vision of the future? There is a generalized perception among younger people today that the future will be no better (socially and economically) than that of previous generations. It is a reality that European countries weigh on the scales of history in the twenty-first century much less than in the twentieth century. In this sense this is true: There is a lack of vision of the future. But it is also true that we are living in a period of strong emotions. The French political scientist Dominique Moïsi even talked about the "geopolitics of emotion," going so far as to analyze the importance of emotions in our politics today.

What are our emotions though? Among the most current ones I would include fear, an ancient feeling so topical in the boundless world of globalization. Fear corrodes the desire and hope to be able to work on visions because it rejects them in the present, making one defensive. Visions require hope, imagination, risk, faith, trust, and an investment in the future....Our societies are full of fear, a feeling that certain politicians know how to use well. Zygmunt Bauman talked about liquid fear, like a demon lurking in the folds of society. This is so much so that one wonders if it is not, at least for Europe, one of the main feelings that accompany global history. Fear does not need visions or prophecies or utopias; on the contrary, it fears them because of their destabilizing tension. Fear demands reassurance, consolation, and defense.

Then there is anger, which for Pankaj Mishra becomes the interpretive key in the *Age of Anger*.[237] Let us not overlook the pages, which I thoroughly agree with, on the inflammatory appeal of victimhood, which pollutes European societies. Despite the problems and widespread discontent, European societies today are not as miserable or insecure as they were in the past or as are others in the world today. The absence of vision, combined with fear, has progressively generated a strong sense of the impossible. However, above all there is the need to defend oneself against a world which has become too big and invasive. Here in particular, the idea of the "wall" was born or reborn.

The concept of a wall seemed to have been swept away by world history after 1989, with the fall of the Berlin Wall, the end of communism, and of the division of Europe into two blocs.[238] We all remember the exciting images of the fall of the Berlin Wall that introduced the period of globalization with such enthusiasm, as if we were faced with a season of great unifying processes. There were still the walls inherited from the Cold War, for example between the two Koreas, or in Nicosia on the island of Cyprus.

"Wall of the impossible," in the title of this chapter, is an evocative expression referring to new material and immaterial barriers. However, I realize that I have talked a lot about vision and not much about walls, whereas this is a reality of today. It is a paralyzing barrier, a cultural, human, and social fact. It is also an aspiration to desire more protection. The wall of the impossible is inside minds and hearts, in cultures, and in discourse. There is also a wall that makes it impos-

---

237. Mishra, *Age of Anger*.
238. The wall had been built in 1961 to stop East Berliners from going to the West. It has been defined as "a barrier for anti-fascist protection." The term "Iron Curtain" was coined by Churchill and used since 1946.

sible to go any further. In the last years we have witnessed the construction of defensive walls, obstructing access for refugees and immigrants from some European countries, a situation in contradiction with global population flows.

Since 2015, there has been a wall separating Hungary from Serbia to stop the refugees traveling north through the Balkans. A Brazilian newspaper, *"Folha de São Paulo,"* calculated that in 2001 there were fifteen walls—today seventy—built to stop immigrants or to hide the poor. In the 1990s, the United States built a wall along the Mexican border to stop the pressure of immigration from the south. In Ceuta in Morocco, one can see Spain's wall. One could go on to show how the global world is a "world of walls." The wall shows the willingness to not share a space with the other who is feared; but above all, it is the desire to isolate oneself from what is on the other side of the wall: people, immigrants, threats, instability ...

Globalization, through so much information, throws us into the depths of history. Mircea Eliade said, "Man living in a certain time is defenseless in the face of history." Yet never has he had so many resources, so much freedom and possibilities. It almost seems as though this freedom has made him insecure. This topic has been addressed by two scholars of Jewish origin, each with a different approach: Emmanuel Lévinas, a philosopher who died in 1995 and Abraham Heschel, who died in 1972, a philosopher who concentrated in particular on prophetism and Jewish spirituality. Lévinas saw that insecurity was typical of freedom.[239] On the other

---

239. Cfr. Michaël de Saint-Cheron, *Entretiens avec Emmanuel Levinas 1992-1994*, (Paris: Librairie Génerale Française, 2006); Giovanni Ferretti, *Emmanuel Levinas: Un profilo e quattro temi teologici*, (Brescia: Queriniana, 2016).

hand, Heschel wrote, "The true essence of freedom is the ability to go beyond oneself."[240]

The truth is that walls suffocate us. How will those European countries which do not want to take in immigrants cope with the problems of their decrease in population? We grow old behind the wall.... That is just one example. At a cultural and personal level, the absence of encounters or dialogue suffocates us. There is a lack of a drive to go beyond, to look for a vision. That is why there is a need for culture and encounters to prepare us for the global world. Our Italian society needs to invest in culture. It is not possible to live in a complex society like ours without questioning, discussing, and reading. Simplifications and fears are rooted in ignorance.

The Turkish author Ferit Edgű's novel, *Un inverno ad Hakkâri* ("A winter in Hakkâri") is about a young teacher, sent to teach in an inland region of Turkey where he does not feel at ease.[241] The young man meets an elderly Syriac Christian bookseller (a survivor of a world long gone) who sells him some books, saying, "Here, I've given you ten books to become your ten friends." The teacher read them and even in his isolation, he gained a new sense of reality. Books as friends and culture, and friendship in an encounter. Unfortunately, the bookshop was burned down by Islamic fanatics and the bookseller disappeared.

An Iranian Kurdish mystic, Malek, an extraordinary woman who died in 1993, wrote in a poem:

> O friends, never be alone, not even for a moment,
> seek companions with minds similar to yours, in harmony with you....

---

240. Abraham Joshua Heschel, *Il canto della libertà: La vita interiore e la liberazione dell'uomo*, (Magnano: Qiqajon, 1999), p. 48.
241. Ferit Edgu, *Un inverno a Hakkari*, ed. Carlo Guarrera (Messina: Mesogea, 2009).

A heavy burden is neither lifted nor carried alone. Many must unite to distribute the load and share it.[242]

Cultivating visions is culture, historical memory, encounters, friendship, dialogue— a horizon on which to organize the news and manage the media and social media by trying to place them in a series of categories. Vision is a drive toward freedom. It means experiencing history again; it means going beyond walls toward the land of the impossible. However, in order to experience this, it is necessary to start talking and meeting again, not just clashing or ignoring each other. In his speech at the United Nations, Umberto Eco said, "In a world in which we are tempted to forget or ignore, reclaiming our collective past should be one of the most important projects of our future."[243] Reclaiming the past and affirming a dialogical dimension of life are the grounds on which visions of the future mature. Moreover, when one reclaims history, one sees the horrors of past wars and understands the value of peace. This confirms the aspiration for peace, which can become an inspiring vision of personal action, of politics, of the future.

---

242. Leili Anvar-Chenderoff and Antonella Anedda, *Malek Jan Ne'mati. La vita non è breve ma il nostro tempo è limitato* (Rome: Empiria, 2010).
243. Umberto Eco, *Contro la perdita della memoria,* lecture delivered at the United Nations (New York, October 21, 2013). Umberto_Eco_ONU_2013_Contro_la_perdita_della_memoria.pdf (festivalcomunicazione.it) See English translation online LEZIONE DEL PROF. UMBERTO ECO ALL'ONU IN NEW YORK SU "CONTRO LA PERDITA DELLA MEMORIA" (21 ottobre 2013) – Rappresentanza Permanente d'Italia ONU – New York (esteri.it)

FOCOLARE MEDIA
Enkindling the Spirit of Unity

The New City Press book you are holding in your hands is one of the many resources produced by Focolare Media, which is a ministry of the Focolare Movement in North America. The Focolare is a worldwide community of people who feel called to bring about the realization of Jesus' prayer: "That all may be one" (see John 17:21).

Focolare Media wants to be your primary resource for connecting with people, ideas, and practices that build unity. Our mission is to provide content that empowers people to grow spiritually, improve relationships, engage in dialogue, and foster collaboration within the Church and throughout society.

 Visit www.focolaremedia.com to learn more about all of New City Press's books, our award-winning magazine *Living City*, videos, podcasts, events, and free resources.

www.ingramcontent.com/pod-product-compliance
Lightning Source LLC
Chambersburg PA
CBHW071417160426
43195CB00013B/1722